The Hundred Years' War

A Captivating Guide to One of the Most Notable Conflicts of the Middle Ages and in European History and the Life of Joan of Arc

© Copyright 2019

All Rights Reserved. No part of this book may be reproduced in any form without permission in writing from the author. Reviewers may quote brief passages in reviews.

Disclaimer: No part of this publication may be reproduced or transmitted in any form or by any means, mechanical or electronic, including photocopying or recording, or by any information storage and retrieval system, or transmitted by email without permission in writing from the publisher.

While all attempts have been made to verify the information provided in this publication, neither the author nor the publisher assumes any responsibility for errors, omissions or contrary interpretations of the subject matter herein.

This book is for entertainment purposes only. The views expressed are those of the author alone, and should not be taken as expert instruction or commands. The reader is responsible for his or her own actions.

Adherence to all applicable laws and regulations, including international, federal, state and local laws governing professional licensing, business practices, advertising and all other aspects of doing business in the US, Canada, UK or any other jurisdiction is the sole responsibility of the purchaser or reader.

Neither the author nor the publisher assumes any responsibility or liability whatsoever on the behalf of the purchaser or reader of these materials. Any perceived slight of any individual or organization is purely unintentional.

Free Bonus from Captivating History (Available for a Limited time)

Hi History Lovers!

Now you have a chance to join our exclusive history list so you can get your first history ebook for free as well as discounts and a potential to get more history books for free! Simply visit the link below to join.

Captivatinghistory.com/ebook

Also, make sure to follow us on Facebook, Twitter and Youtube by searching for Captivating History.

Table of Contents

PART 1: THE HUNDRED YEARS' WAR 1
   INTRODUCTION 2
   SECTION ONE: THE EDWARDIAN WAR (1337-1360) 4
   CHAPTER 1 - A QUESTION OF SUCCESSION 5
   CHAPTER 2 - STRIKING THE FIRST BLOW 10
   CHAPTER 3 - DEATH OF A DIFFERENT ILK 16
   CHAPTER 4 - THE BLACK PRINCE'S RAID 23
   CHAPTER 5 - THE TREATY OF BRÉTIGNY 30
   SECTION TWO: THE CAROLINE WAR (1369-1389) 36
   CHAPTER 6 - CHARLES THE WISE 37
   CHAPTER 7 - THE DEATH OF JOHN CHANDOS 42
   CHAPTER 8 - A FRENCH VICTORY 48
   CHAPTER 9 - THE GREAT CHEVAUCHÉE 53
   CHAPTER 10 - TWO BOY KINGS 58
   CHAPTER 11 - MADNESS AND DEPOSITION 65
   SECTION THREE: THE LANCASTRIAN WAR (1415-1453) 71
   CHAPTER 12 - BESIEGING HARFLEUR 72
   CHAPTER 13 - THE BATTLE OF AGINCOURT 78

CHAPTER 14 - A BABY KING 84
CHAPTER 15 - JOAN AND THE SIEGE.. 90
CHAPTER 16 - THE LAST BATTLES 96
CONCLUSION.. 101
APPENDIX: COMPREHENSIVE TIMELINE OF THE
HUNDRED YEARS' WAR 103
PART 2: JOAN OF ARC 108
INTRODUCTION 109
CHAPTER 1 - THE UNENDING WAR.. 111
CHAPTER 2 - A WHISPERED PROPHECY....................................... 116
CHAPTER 3 - THE FIRST VISION 122
CHAPTER 4 - THE DOUBT OF BAUDRICOURT 127
CHAPTER 5 - A PREDICTION OF DEFEAT..................................... 133
CHAPTER 6 - AN AUDIENCE WITH THE KING......................... 139
CHAPTER 7 - THE ROAD TO ORLÉANS 144
CHAPTER 8 - ARRIVAL AT ORLÉANS 149
CHAPTER 9 - FLYING THE WHITE BANNER 153
CHAPTER 10 - A SIGN PROVIDED.. 158
CHAPTER 11 - THE BATTLE OF PATAY... 163
CHAPTER 12 - BEANS FOR THE APOCALYPSE............................ 168
CHAPTER 13 - THE FRENCH KING CROWNED.......................... 173
CHAPTER 14 - THE SIEGE OF PARIS 177
CHAPTER 15 - PEACE... 182
CHAPTER 16 - CAPTURE 186
CHAPTER 17 - CAPTIVE.. 191
CHAPTER 18 - A SAINT TRIED FOR HERESY 196
CHAPTER 19 - THE BURNING OF JEANNE D'ARC..................... 201
CONCLUSION.. 204
HERE'S ANOTHER BOOK BY CAPTIVATING HISTORY
THAT YOU MIGHT LIKE... 208
FREE BONUS FROM CAPTIVATING HISTORY
(AVAILABLE FOR A LIMITED TIME) 209
SOURCES.. 210

Part 1: The Hundred Years' War

A Captivating Guide to the Conflicts Between the English House of Plantagenet and the French House of Valois That Took Place During the Middle Ages

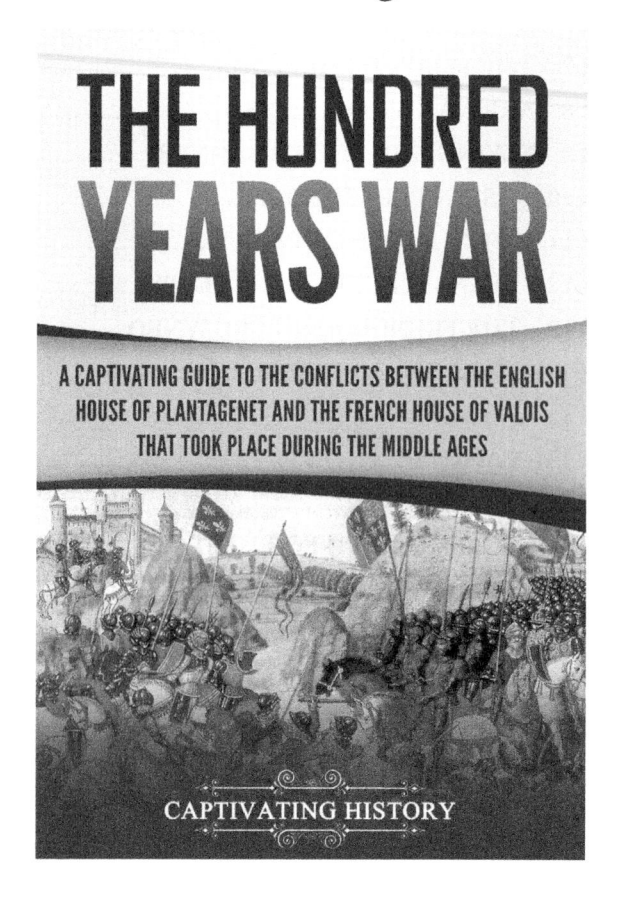

Introduction

Knights and battles, princesses and castles, sieges and warrior prophets who lead the way to victory upon shining white horses: all of these feel like the stuff of myths and legends. Yet the story of the Hundred Years' War contains all of these things, and it is a story that is entirely true.

Nearly seven hundred years ago, France and England were both ruled by warrior kings who led their own troops into battle. It was a time of turmoil and terror, a time when the Black Death stalked the streets and the drama of two specific families could cause continental war. It was a time known as the Dark Ages, and yet the modern imagination can't help but find itself captivated by the romance of a time when chivalry was a code used in war.

The story of this war is made fascinating by its setting, but it is made inspiring by its characters. Here is a blind king who rides to war for the opportunity to strike one last blow with his sword; here is a young prince, dressed all in black, who leads his father's men to victory; here are boy kings and fierce queens, prisoners who believe in honor, hailstorms that stop entire campaigns, and the wonderful story of a young peasant girl who changed the course of history forever.

The Hundred Years' War changed language, national identity, weaponry, and even the way that people think about war. It is part of the greater narrative of human history and gives a snapshot of how human nature can behave when pressed by the extremity of such a conflict—sometimes with unspeakable honor and courage and other times with cowardice, selfishness, and arrogance. There are many lessons to be learned from this war. Its tale is a cautionary one, but it is also a tale of adventure, battle, hope, and divine intervention. It's the tale of a war unlike any other.

Section One:
The Edwardian War (1337-1360)

Chapter 1 – A Question of Succession

The queen of France was only eighteen, but this would be her third child. Tears poured down her smooth cheeks as she panted and screamed in her luxurious bedchamber, attended by a pale-faced midwife and a band of panicking female servants. Queen Jeanne d'Évreux ignored them, gritting her teeth over the wave of agony that came with another contraction. Hope and fear clashed in her heart as the young queen strained to bring her child into the world. Jeanne had been through so much even at her age. Married to King Charles IV at the tender age of fourteen, she had already lost her first baby and, just two months ago, her husband. Now she knew that the fate of the entire kingdom was waiting in this room, hinged on the gender of the baby that she was about to deliver.

Jeanne had given Charles two children before he died. The first, named after her mother, had lived only a few months. The second was strong and healthy so far, but also a daughter. Now Charles was dead and left behind neither brothers nor sons. If the French Crown was to remain in the hands of the House of Capet, this baby had to be a boy. Otherwise, there were two main claimants to the throne. One was Charles IV's first cousin, Philip of Valois, who was already serving as regent; the other was Edward III, the King of England. France could not fall into his hands.

Finally, relief. Jeanne fell back onto her pillows, sweat soaking the sheets as the midwife lifted the baby. There was a beat of silence that made Jeanne's heart freeze. Then, a thin cry rose into the air, filling the chamber with the sound of a new life.

Exhausted and awash with pain, Jeanne still managed to ask the baby's gender. The midwife looked at her with wide eyes, knowing full well the importance of the question. But there was no denying the truth.

Jeanne had given birth to another baby girl. Charles IV had no heir.

* * * *

It was 1328, and France and England had been chafing at one another for centuries. Ever since William the Conqueror had landed at Hastings and destroyed the English king in 1066, infusing English royalty with French blood, the two great kingdoms had been butting heads. The most recent struggle had been the brief War of Saint-Sardos when Charles IV and King Edward II of England had struggled for control over a small province on the west coast of France named Gascony. William the Conqueror had been Duke of Normandy; through his lineage, the king of England continued to have territories in France, and although France gradually won back most of its land, Gascony remained under the control of the English king. This meant that the king of England owed homage to the king of France. Homage was a symbolic ritual in which a person who owned land in a region presided over by a higher-ranking person would pledge allegiance and submission to their lord; in this case, the king of England was also Duke of Aquitaine (including Gascony), and he thus had to pay homage to the king of France.

This did not sit at all well with any of the English kings, and multiple attempts were made to seize Gascony entirely from France. Philip VI's father, Charles of Valois, had recently defeated English King Edward II in a struggle over Gascony.

It was supposed to be a gesture of peace when Charles IV's sister Isabella of France married Edward II. Instead, it would spark the longest-lasting European conflict in history.

Ancient Salic Law, which had been adopted by the French courts, prevented women from inheriting titles; for this reason, Jeanne's two daughters Marie and the newborn Blanche were ineligible for Charles IV's title. Instead, Charles IV's paternal first cousin Philip VI was crowned king of France.

However, England was about to throw a wrench in the works once again. Isabella of France was more successful in producing heirs than Queen Jeanne had been. By the time Charles IV died, Isabella's son Edward III was king of England. As Charles IV's nephew, he was the deceased king's closest male relative and technically could lay a claim to the throne, which he briskly did when Philip VI was crowned. The French court, however, argued that since Isabella had no right to the throne, she couldn't pass that same right on to Edward. The French were deeply reluctant to be ruled by an Englishman and clung to this reason for not allowing Edward to gain the throne. Reluctantly, Edward realized that he had lost this particular battle. To continue to dispute the French court's decision would lead to war, and Edward was only seventeen years old when he took the throne; war on France at that stage was a mistake even a teenage king knew would be too costly to make.

Thus, in 1329, the young king paid homage to Philip VI, a gesture that utterly invalidated his claim to the throne. The homage ceremony was simple but profoundly humiliating. The tenant would be stripped of his weaponry and any crowns or other jewelry signifying his rank; he would then approach the lord, who would be seated, and go down on both knees. Placing his folded hands in between the hands of the lord, he would swear a simple oath of allegiance. The lord would accept the tenant's oath by means of a kiss.

But Edward III did not plan to abase himself so completely. When he strode into the throne room of King Philip VI, he was resplendently adorned with his glittering crown and his mighty broadsword sheathed at his hip. Philip watched in simmering silence as the young king approached, his eyes intent, his posture indicating everything but submission. It was almost a surprise when Edward sank to his knees before the French throne and placed his hands in Philip's. "I become your man from this day forward," he declared formally, but the eyes that bored into Philip's were filled with defiance, "and unto you shall be true and faithful, and bear to you faith for the tenements that I claim to hold of you, saving the faith that I owe to our sovereign lord." He paused, lifting his chin, making it abundantly clear of whom he was speaking. "The king."

Philip VI studied Edward for a long, perilous moment. Then he consented to bend down and accept the oath with a kiss. Edward stalked out, his head held high. Homage was paid, but the entire room could feel the chill of how meaningless the gesture was.

* * * *

The homage ceremony, as unusual and tense as it was, was still good enough to buy Europe a few more years of peace. Edward continued to pay homage to Philip as was required, but trouble was still brewing through another key player in this dangerous chess game of medieval politics. This was Robert III of Artois. Robert was a relative of King Philip VI and had been instrumental in getting him onto the throne; moreover, he became one of Philip's closest advisers. Yet this position of power was not enough for him. He wanted more land, and he felt he was entitled to the County of Artois itself. It was under the control of his aunt Mahaut, Countess of Artois, but he presented a forged document discussing his father's will to King Philip, hoping that his ally, the king, wouldn't look too closely. His hopes were dashed when Philip realized that the document was a forgery; Robert's lands were confiscated, and he was driven out of France as a disgrace and an exile. He hid in Namur and later Brabant.

Meanwhile, Philip VI was occupied with more than just hounding the treacherous Robert. He knew what Edward's defiance at the homage ceremony meant—that the ceremony hadn't been a declaration of peace, just a delaying of inevitable war. He began to gather allies that could help him in the conflict, and one of the most important of these allies was Scotland. Perpetually at war with England, the Scots needed support, and Philip knew that if England could be caught between two enemies, they would be hard-pressed to win. He formed an alliance with Edward's sworn enemy, King David II of Scotland.

Enraged, Edward sought means for retaliation. And when Philip invaded Brabant and drove Robert out of his haven once more, the deceitful adviser became an ideal way to goad the French king. Edward welcomed Robert into his court, not only harboring the fugitive but making him one of his own advisers as well. Robert had a bone to pick with Philip, and he urged Edward to stir up trouble against France, wanting the two countries to go to war. Perhaps that way he would finally get Artois.

It worked. Robert was the last straw. Edward abruptly stopped paying homage to Philip at all, and in April 1337, diplomatic relations ceased and the call to arms was sounded all over France. Philip confiscated Gascony, citing Edward's lack of homage and the harboring of Robert as good reason. Edward's next move was to lay another claim to the French throne, and all the old reasons for France and England to be at war flared up once again.

The inevitable conflict had begun. Yet none of the combatants could possibly have guessed at how long it would endure—and how high a price both countries would pay.

Chapter 2 – Striking the First Blow

Illustration I: A medieval cog

The two knights were not optimistic. Still sweating in their heavy armor after their brisk ride, they stood before their king with dubious expressions, trying their best to convey their message without angering the king.

But they knew it was too late. Edward III was an angry man, a man who had spent the past three years trying to gather funding and support for the war he had—perhaps unwisely—declared on his neighboring country. While war had officially been declared in April 1337, only small skirmishes had taken place for several months while both Edward III and Philip VI tried to find the necessary funding for war. For Edward, this was an uphill battle. While Philip had a massive fleet of warships—swift galleys from Castile, elegant, maneuverable, and designed for battle—Edward had only three warships to his name. He was forced to scrape together an assortment of cogs, wallowing merchant vessels that could carry large amounts of men but at a slow speed. They were made for neither swiftness nor agility, and it showed.

Still, Edward could commission hundreds of them, taking them from merchants, often without compensating them, and built defensive ramparts known as "castles" in front and behind the massive mast that stood amidships. His particular pride and joy was one such redesigned cog, a massive and majestic thing named the *Christopher*. She could carry vast numbers of fighters or cargo, and better yet, she was equipped with the wondrous new weapons that had just been invented: artillery. No longer was Edward forced to use pulleys, levers, and counterweights to launch rocks at his enemies from crude trebuchets and catapults. Now, he had cannons, some of the very first of their kind, magical things that blew metal balls into the ranks of his enemies simply by lighting a fuse.

The *Christopher* had three such cannons on board, and so, in September 1338, she was sent to the island of Walcheren near the County of Flanders (an English ally on the coast of France) to guard a huge cargo of wool that Edward was sending to his allies. He hoped that by trading this great shipment of wool with the Flemish, he would not only strengthen diplomatic relations with them but also raise some much-needed funds in order to employ and equip his army. His hopes were horribly dashed when the fast-moving French fleet descended upon the *Christopher* and her companions like an angel of death. There were forty-eight French galleys surrounding the five English cogs, and the English simply didn't stand a chance. Commander John Kingston held them off for a full day before he was forced to surrender, and the French sailed triumphantly back to their king with a rich booty and Edward's precious *Christopher* in tow.

This loss at the Battle of Arnemuiden was a sucker punch to Edward's gut, especially after his port city of Portsmouth had been ransacked and burned to the ground in March 1338. It took Edward almost two years to do it, but he painstakingly put together a fleet, threw back the French, and was now on the offensive. Sailing across the channel with 150 ships, Edward was determined to strike back, to overwhelm the French navy and take one of their ports. And their presence at Flanders was an insult both to him and to the Flemish, most of whom were decidedly allied to the English king since Philip VI had been treating them poorly.

Now, on June 24th, 1340, Edward was waiting aboard his own cog, the *Thomas*, for word from two knights that he'd sent to scout out the harbor of Sluys. The city was located on the coast of Flanders, and its massive harbor was one of the key trading points between England and its ally of Flanders. The French knew this and had set their battle in array at the mouth of the harbor. Drawing three lines of their ships across the mouth, they had mustered an incredible fleet, backed up by their allies from Genoa and Castile. The two knights told the king as much, shaking their heads in disappointment. The quarters were just too close, they said; to attack those agile galleys in a narrow space with waddling, ponderous cogs would be foolish. A wise king would wait.

But Edward was not wise just yet. At twenty-seven years old, he was far from the rebellious teenager who had paid homage to Philip

VI wearing a blade and a crown, but he was still prone to fly into fits of rage and make questionable decisions. This was one of those times. When he looked up at the two knights as they finished their report, the flames of Portsmouth were ablaze in his eyes. His shouting echoed around the *Thomas* as he ordered the knights out and called his men to arms—they were attacking Sluys, and there were no two ways about it.

* * * *

The ensuing battle was one of the bloodiest of the Middle Ages. Edward's force was mighty, but as he stood on the deck of the *Thomas* to approach the French fleet, their masts protruding through the mist looked—as historians would later describe them—like a forest floating on the sea. But when they drew closer, the English king laughed with scorn because he knew that the battle was his. Those swift galleys had two great advantages over his cogs—their agility and speed—and they had cast both advantages to the wind. The French commanders, Hugues Quiéret and Nicolas Béhuchet, had opted to array their ships in two lines across the mouth of the harbor and then lash them together with boarding lines. This made the line of ships sturdy and allowed men-at-arms to hurry from one ship to the next, but it also made them virtually immovable. All that French maneuverability was gone. Galley after galley was tied to its neighbor, with the *Christopher*, that stolen English cog, looming among them like an ox among sheep.

Edward sent his ships forward in three lines: one cog loaded with ample men-at-arms that carried weapons for close combat flanked by two more that carried England's legendary longbowmen. These lightly-armored soldiers carried mighty bows, many of them as long or longer than the men were tall, usually carved of one single piece of yew. The longbow was a magnificently elegant, simple object, yet capable of launching a steel-tipped arrow as far as three hundred yards with deadly force. The longbowmen had all grown up with archery, using it for hunting and recreation until they could shoot with unrivaled accuracy. As the ships filled with bowmen lumbered up to the French line, volley after volley of arrows flew into the French ships, wreaking havoc. Sails were torn down, and men screamed and splashed into the water as the longbows punctured mail and even plate armor. By the time the cog filled with men-at-arms reached the French line, it was in chaos. The Englishmen boarded and attacked with devastating efficiency. In a panic, many of the French leaped from their ships, seeking refuge in the sea, only to be washed up on the shores of Flanders and attacked by hundreds of club-wielding angry Flemish.

The death toll was unprecedented. Edward would later write to his son, the Black Prince, of how bodies continued to wash up on the French shore for days. The harbor's water was tinged in scarlet, the French fleet destroyed, and the *Christopher* and her sister the *Edward* were recaptured into English hands. The Battle of Sluys was the first major engagement of the Hundred Years' War, and it was a most decisive victory for Edward, so much so that France panicked and expected a full-scale invasion for control over the entirety of France, not just Edward's bid to lay claim to Gascony. As many as 20,000 Frenchmen were killed; Edward's casualties are unknown but likely very few.

As decisive as the victory was at Sluys, it did not have as great of a tactical effect as Edward was hoping for. While he was able to lay siege to the city of Tournai, Edward had not solved the problem of Philip VI's running cargo across the English Channel to Scotland's King David II, Edward's oldest enemy. Nor did the raids of port towns on the English coast cease; Philip's greater resources allowed him to swiftly put his navy back together, and by the end of the year, he was pillaging English towns once more.

Edward's coffers, however, did not refill quite so quickly. As the French continued to cripple England's wool trade—one of its major incomes—Edward stubbornly clung to his siege of Tournai. As Edward's funds drained, so did the food supplies of the inhabitants of the city and the French garrison stationed there. Both sides were getting equally desperate as the weeks wore on; by September 1340, three months after the siege commenced, Edward was practically penniless, and Tournai was starving. It was at this point that Jeanne de Valois, Philip's sister and Edward's mother-in-law, decided to intervene. She brought an impassioned plea before the warring kings, asking them to bring peace to two nations that had lost thousands of people in the war already. Both kings, knowing they were on the brink of defeat, begrudgingly agreed to sign the Truce of Espléchin on September 25th, 1340. The truce stipulated peace for five years and sent Edward and his army marching back to England before winter could strike with her fullest fury.

The peace, however, was short-lived. A contested succession would once again set France alight with war. John III the Good, Duke of Brittany, died in April 1341; he had married three times yet had no heir. He left behind a half-brother named John of Montfort, but John the Good had no interest in leaving the duchy to him—Montfort's mother was John the Good's hated stepmother. Instead, the Duke's niece's husband, Charles of Blois, decided that the duchy was rightfully his. Philip VI backed Charles, and Montfort resolved to go to war. Edward saw his chance and flung his renewed resources behind Montfort, and so the War of the Breton Succession broke out, destroying the truce and becoming the first of many proxy wars that would be fought during the Hundred Years' War.

Chapter 3 – Death of a Different Ilk

The War of the Breton Succession was the perfect excuse for Edward and Philip to come to blows once more. Edward continued to back John of Montfort in Brittany and to push against French campaigns in Gascony, as Philip fiercely resisted. The drawn-out struggle in Brittany continued with few decisive battles on either side. Major cities like Vannes and Nantes were repeatedly besieged and changed hands multiple times, and for the next five years, the struggle seemed to have no real direction.

The most ironic fact about the War of the Breton Succession is that Edward III—heir to the throne of France through the female line—was supporting John of Montfort, heir to the Duchy of Brittany through the male line. Likewise, Philip was supporting Charles of Blois, whose claim to the duchy was similar to Edward's claim to the throne. It leaves little doubt in one's mind that these two kings were looking for reasons to go to war much more than they were actually interested in the events in Brittany.

At any rate, the war in Brittany kept them occupied with small battles for five years, allowing Edward to replenish his failing funds and rebuild the army that had been drained of its resources at Tournai. By July 1346, Edward had amassed a force that he hoped could win back some land for England at last. The war had been raging for almost a decade, and Edward was still determined that France would be his. Or, if he couldn't take it during his lifetime, then it would at least belong to his heir—Prince Edward of Woodstock. The lad was only sixteen years old at the time, but King Edward was determined for him to prove himself in battle, and when the English force landed on the shores of the Cotentin Peninsula, Prince Edward was one of its commanders.

The aim of this force—numbering some 15,000 men—was to execute a chevauchée. This popular tactic was commonly used to weaken the resources of an enemy kingdom. In a chevauchée, the army would avoid engaging any fortified towns or armies, instead moving across the countryside and setting fire to villages or pillaging towns in order to destroy resources that the enemy would have used for war. While peasants generally were not purposely slaughtered, those who resisted were mercilessly cut down, and their homes and fields burnt to the ground. King Edward executed this tactic with a vengeance, remembering the plundering of English ports, and his horsemen swept across the countryside destroying all in their path. Town after town fell before them like wheat before the scythe, and many of these rich Normandy towns were ripe for the harvest; the English carried off mountains of wealth.

Finally, after destroying Normandy's capital of Caen, King Edward swung his force toward the River Seine and aimed for Paris. When this happened, Philip had finally had enough. He mustered a troop of almost 20,000 men—consisting of his magnificent cavalry and a group of Genoese mercenaries—and headed to attack the English. Seeing that his battle had rapidly turned from an invasion to a defense, Edward placed his army on the steep slope of a hill at

Crécy-en-Ponthieu and waited.

On August 26th, 1346, the French knights thundered through the countryside, aglitter in armor on their great, sweating horses. These were some of the best cavalries in Europe, and cavalry was the heart of medieval warfare. Heavily armored in strong steel plates and meticulous chainmail, these knights were virtually impenetrable; they carried long, powerful lances that could pierce through practically anything in a charge, and were also armed with long swords that were deadly in a fight. Their horses were majestic creatures, agile and powerful, many of them even trained to kick and bite their enemies; they were also armored with metal plates known as barding. The French warhorses, known as destriers, were particularly fine. These muscular animals were also fresh and full of energy; a knight seldom actually rode his destrier from one place to another. Instead, he would ride a less valuable animal while his squire followed, leading the destrier. Englishmen often used less valuable coursers—fast-moving and spirited horses that were not as strong or beautiful as the destrier.

These knights on their mighty chargers were the pride of the French army, and they were complemented by some of the finest mercenaries in Europe. Genoese crossbowmen were highly skilled with their crossbows, weapons which were capable of launching heavy bolts over long distances and with great force. Crossbows were slower to load than longbows, however, and for this reason, crossbowmen were also equipped with a pavise—a large, rectangular shield—to duck behind as they loaded their weapons.

From the ranks of his father's army, Prince Edward watched in trepidation as the mighty French force approached. His father had made a controversial decision to dismount all of his knights and station them in a solid block with some other men-at-arms, effectively taking away their greatest advantage, their horses. But he had once again employed the tactic that had been so successful at Sluys: he had flanked the block of infantry with a V-shape, known as a harrow, of archers. Their ranks bristled with longbows as they waited for the French to come within range, and Prince Edward knew that as strong as the French armor was, the force of an arrow from a longbow was enough to pierce it.

Still, he couldn't help but feel a little nervous. Prince Edward was only sixteen, yet he was commanding one of his father's three blocks of infantry flanked by archers. In fact, he was commanding the vanguard—the group, or "battle," of men that were closest to the enemy—while his father was behind him, with the Earl of Northampton in the rear. He had not yet been part of any major battles, but Prince Edward now found himself facing a charge of French knights thundering up the hillside toward him. His courage faltered for a second, but he did not let it show. Flinging himself to the front of the line, Prince Edward rallied his men with a cry, his black armor vivid in the fading light as the Frenchmen charged. The Genoese crossbowmen launched the first of their missiles, and the English longbowmen responded with a volley of arrows that fell like deadly rain upon the French. As the arrows punched into the Genoese line, Prince Edward saw with a thrill of excitement that the Genoese did not have their pavises—they had left them on the French baggage train. The knights had no backup; they plunged directly toward the English infantry with no protection against the longbowmen, and their charge was mowed down by the rain of arrows, knights falling in all directions. The handful of horsemen that got through to Prince Edward's army were sliced down by polearms and swords. Prince Edward's line barely faltered. The great cavalry charge had been a failure.

King Philip was watching as the common English longbows destroyed the elite of the French. Enraged, he blamed the Genoese archers, who were fleeing from the longbows. He turned to his knights. "Kill those scoundrels!" he snapped. "They stop up our road without any reason."

Obediently, one detachment of knights fell upon the mercenaries, butchering them mercilessly while their comrades continued to attack the English. Yet the English line held despite the might of the French cavalry. At one point, Prince Edward's battle came under heavy pressure, but his father declined to help him. "Let the boy win his spurs!" he cried, and the boy did, beating his enemies and putting them to flight.

The French cavalry would go on to charge as many as sixteen times that night. Every time, they were repulsed by those longbowmen. The French dead continued to pile up, while the English were losing hardly any men at all. Philip himself played at the very edges of death; twice his horses were shot out from under him, and twice he rose again. It was only when he was shot in the jaw with an arrow that the French king finally admitted defeat. He retreated, and the next morning, a handful of English longbowmen chased the last of the French army into the hills.

Prince Edward was immediately famous. The young man was a champion of the battle and immediately became a hero of his people. He became legendary for his courage and for the black armor he wore at Crécy, which gave him the title of Edward the Black Prince, a name that would be engraved in the soul of chivalry.

But there was one enemy to whom the Black Prince wished to pay his respects, and that was John, the king of Bohemia. John was stone blind and aging, and he knew that one way or another, Crécy was going to be his last battle. He asked his retinue to guide him into the fighting so that he could just strike one last blow and die on his own terms, not alone and in the darkness. They did as he asked, and he fell with them all, dead on the battlefield, just as he had wanted. According to legend, out of respect for his valiant opponent, the Black Prince took John's emblem and motto—*I Serve*—for his own.

* * * *

The Battle of Crécy would go down in history as one of the very few medieval battles where infantry could hope to stand against cavalry. This was in large part due to the prowess of the English longbowmen. Once again, King Edward III had proven his capability as a military commander, particularly in his use of archers. The French were mortified to see so many of their knights—which were commonly the nobility—killed by commoners wielding longbows.

It was also another battle in which the earliest form of a cannon was used. While these cannons likely did not inflict many casualties and were fairly insignificant compared to the longbowmen, their presence did terrify the French, and they did use gunpowder to fire their missiles. This made it one of the first major European battles during which guns were used.

This battle allowed King Edward to move his army on to the fortified city of Calais, to which they promptly laid siege and defeated the following year. Calais became a cornerstone of the English invasion and would remain under the control of the English for more than a century, even after the Hundred Years' War was over.

But King Edward's offensive did not last as long as he hoped. Promising as it started, in 1348, a common enemy would rise up against the two warring kings, a struggle so mighty that it completely distracted them from the war and forced them to focus merely on survival. The plague had arrived in France.

This pandemic of bubonic plague—known as the Black Death—was one of the greatest tragedies that Europe has ever suffered. Transmitted by fleas that were common on house rats at the time, the bacterium *Yersinia pestis* caused death within three to seven days in over sixty percent of its victims. With no understanding of how the disease was being transmitted, the people of medieval Europe could do nothing to stop it and little to treat it; it swept through the continent with devastating speed, killing as many as fifty million people between 1346 and 1353. With such a formidable enemy to face, war had to be forgotten. Thousands upon thousands died; mass graves were layered with human bodies, and there were hardly enough people left alive to bury the millions of dead.

The social and economic effects of the plague were tremendous. There was certainly no time for the kings to be fighting with human foes when faced with such a terrible opponent. The Hundred Years' War stalled, but the suffering of the European people did not abate until the 1350s. It only came to an end when almost two-thirds of the population was dead. England and France were both economically crippled and slowly set to putting their countries back together after the horrendous decimation of the plague.

Edward III and the Black Prince were both survivors of the plague. And despite the destruction they had just witnessed, neither of them was done with the war. As soon as England could recover, they were going to fight for the throne they believed was rightfully theirs.

Chapter 4 – The Black Prince's Raid

Illustration II: The capture of King John II and his son Philip the Bold at the Battle of Poitiers. Longbows can be seen in the background, as well as the king's battle-ax.

The Black Death had no respect for rank. It swept through Europe killing wherever and whatever it could—peasants, commoners, knights, nobility, and even, in 1350, the king of France.

King Philip VI had already lost his wife and regent, Joan the Lame, in 1349 due to the plague. Ironically, while Philip spent much of his reign fighting the Hundred Years' War in an attempt to protect his throne, Joan was the one who did most of the ruling; she was an indomitable and fiery woman, as intellectual as she was dauntless, and therefore greatly unpopular in an era ruled almost exclusively by men. Still, it was a devastating blow to Philip when Joan died. He followed not long after, claimed, like her, by the terrible plague.

Philip, at least, had succeeded in producing an heir. His oldest son John II—later known as John the Good—was crowned king of France on September 26th, 1350. John II was married to Bonne of Bohemia, the daughter of that courageous and tragic blind king who had been killed at the Battle of Crécy.

Meanwhile, England was recovering from the horrors of the Black Death. Its economy was clawing its way back to stability, and with the pandemic more or less over, King Edward and the Black Prince could turn their thoughts back to the war. King Edward was forging an alliance with the King of Navarre and now had John IV the Conqueror, son of John of Montfort, who was now fighting the War of the Breton Succession at the time, as an ally; he planned to sail to Navarre, but the English nobles in Gascony were complaining of French oppression and hungry for loot, so King Edward decided it was time for another chevauchée. On September 9th, 1355, King Edward sent his son, the Black Prince, to Gascony to renew the attack on France.

Prince Edward had a much smaller force than his father had during the previous chevauchée that had ended in the Battle of Crécy, but he was determined to wreak just as much havoc on the enemy country. With an army of about 6,500 men, consisting of knights, archers, and infantry, the Black Prince took to the countryside and fell upon the towns and villages with a vengeance. Plundering and pillaging wherever he went, he swept across France in eight weeks of destruction. Major cities were sacked, although their fortified citadels were left untouched, and countless treasures were carried off by the Prince and his men. By the time they returned to Bordeaux, they had succeeded in securing a large bounty for England.

In July 1356, almost a year after first setting sail from England, the Black Prince mounted another attack. His plan was to cross France and reach Normandy where he could meet his father and attack King John with their full might. He and his army set forth, once again ransacking every town in their path; notably, this time they attacked fortified cities too. Vierzon fell relatively easily; Romorantin, less so. It might have been wisest to leave Romorantin be, but instead, the Black Prince was blinded by grief after one of his friends had been killed in the fighting. He laid siege to the castle for three days and finally defeated it by using Greek fire—a mysterious compound that burned on contact with water and had been used in warfare since its invention by the Byzantines in the seventh century CE but whose composition has been lost to the mists of time.

The loss of the citadels warned King John of France that real trouble was brewing. He began to amass a large army and arranged it along the banks of the Loire, effectively preventing the Black Prince from being able to reach his allies in Brittany and Navarre. Prince Edward was forced to turn back toward Bordeaux, but he still succeeded in pillaging more towns as he went. However, King John had had enough. Gathering his large force, he followed the Black Prince's trail of destruction, determined to catch up and fight him.

King John II had always been a sickly man. He seldom jousted or hunted, unlike many of the warrior kings of his era; yet he knew that he had to do something in the face of this war, and unlike the political leaders of today, he had to act as general and ride foremost in his ranks if he was to have any credibility among his people. He marched his army as hard as they could go, knowing that they numbered nearly double the Black Prince's force, and determined to catch them before they could reach the city of Poitiers and dig in—which could necessitate a siege.

On September 19th, 1356, King John succeeded in his mission. He came between the English and Poitiers, and now the Black Prince was forced to fight an army 11,000 strong—he only had about 6,000 men at his command. His army ground to a halt, face-to-face with the French, and Prince Edward knew that he was in trouble. He would have to negotiate with the French king in order to avoid a full-on battle.

Negotiations passed back and forth for several hours. Prince Edward offered generous terms: all of the bounties he had seized on his latest chevauchée, as well as a seven-year truce. But it wasn't enough for King John. He demanded that the Black Prince surrender himself and his entire army, which would allow them to be held ransom for a crippling fee that could effectively end the war for England if King Edward would be able to raise the money. And if he didn't, he would have lost one of his most promising commanders and a large chunk of his army. Prince Edward refused the terms and prepared his men for battle. There was going to be no other way.

The Black Prince tucked his soldiers way out in the orchards and hedges of the countryside, concealing his great hope—his two thousand longbowmen—in a thick hedge that flanked the road. The rest of his knights and other soldiers were hidden in the orchards, unbeknownst to King John II, who could see little except the English baggage train. When the Black Prince had the baggage train taken to safety, King John mistook it for an English retreat. He sent three hundred German knights forward to make the first charge and find out where the Black Prince was hiding his men. The knights charged boldly down the road, ready to lay waste to the English, and were met with a rain of arrows that burst from the thick hedge like tiny, zipping messengers of death. The arrows punched through the horse's plate armor, puncturing their backs and hind legs, bringing them down into one another at a full gallop. As the foremost horses fell, they caused the horses behind them to stumble and throw their riders, with the arrows still coming down upon the knights with devastating effect. Hardly any of the Germans survived the onslaught.

Seeing that his cavalry would be useless, King John ordered his men to dismount and march up the road toward the English archers and infantry and attack them on foot. The first column to attack was commanded by King John's oldest son, the Dauphin (heir to the throne) Charles. His men were exhausted by their hard march and stumbled directly into the English trap. Bursting from the hedgerows, the Black Prince's archers and heavy infantry surrounded the Dauphin's forces and briskly overwhelmed them. Tired and defeated, the Dauphin's column fell back and crashed into the second of King John's columns—commanded by the Duke of Orléans—slowing them down and sowing dismay and bewilderment throughout their ranks.

Confused by the Dauphin's retreat, Orléans ordered his men to fall back as well, and in the chaos, the Black Prince saw his chance to see the Frenchmen off. He ordered his knights back onto their horses, and the cavalry surged forward to pursue the fleeing French. As the Black Prince's cavalry punched into the Frenchmen, they were driven right up against King John's column, and heavy fighting began—horsemen facing off against infantry and each other, and the archers casting their mighty longbows aside and setting upon the French with simple close-quarters weapons like daggers and war hammers. King John himself was in the midst of the fight, wielding a mighty battle-ax, but it was not enough. The French army realized that they were at risk of being surrounded and butchered, and in terror, they fled. Only a handful of loyal knights was left fighting in isolated clusters, as well as King John and his youngest son, the fourteen-year-old Philip the Bold.

It was Sir Denis Morbeke of Artois that spotted the king and his courageous little son trying to hold off the English. Sir Denis had been French once but was exiled to England after committing a murder and now fought on the English side; yet his heart went out to King John and the boy, and he decided to extend a hand of mercy to them. Riding up to them, he addressed the King with respect, asking him for his surrender.

Young Philip was clinging to his father's arm, and King John knew that to fight for his honor would cost the life of his child. "To whom shall I yield me?" he asked tiredly. "Where is my cousin, the Prince of Wales? If I might see him, I would speak with him."

Relieved, Sir Denis told him, "Sir, he is not here; but yield you to me and I shall bring you to him."

King John took off his right gauntlet and reluctantly handed it over to the knight. "I yield me to you," he said quietly.

So it was that Sir Denis brought the king and his son safely to the Black Prince, who took them both—and many of the surviving French lords and knights—as prisoner. King John and young Philip were treated well, dining with the Prince in his personal tent, but this did not negate the fact that the French had been decisively defeated. 2,500 Frenchmen had been killed, and a further 1,900 captured; the King was a prisoner, leaving his son Charles, who was only eighteen years old, to govern a country that was ravaged by plague and war. Prince Edward continued on to Bordeaux unopposed and triumphant with significant loot and many prisoners. The English longbowmen had proven themselves once more, although in this case, the Black Prince had used the fear of them to his advantage rather than actually using them to destroy many Frenchmen; it had been the traditional cavalry charge that had truly ended the battle.

France was in utter disarray. The Dauphin Charles attempted to rally his country, but he was met with chaos and resistance. He tried to raise funds to ransom his father by raising taxes, but this was a terrible mistake, as the nobles revolted against him and began to pillage the peasants once again, trying to regain some of the riches that the Black Prince had taken.

English victory had never been closer. But the war was far from over.

Chapter 5 – The Treaty of Brétigny

The Black Prince returned to England triumphant, his ships loaded with French bounty and his most valuable prisoner—King John of France—on board. He was given a hero's welcome, and King John and his captured nobles were all ransomed for millions of crowns—far more than France could ever have raised. For the next several years, King John would remain in captivity, originally in Bordeaux and later in Windsor, England. His imprisonment was by no account a time of great suffering, however. Although the king must have been worried about the chaos into which his country was descending, his needs were all well-tended to. In fact, King John lived in luxury.

Meanwhile, the Dauphin Charles was struggling to maintain some semblance of control over France, and he was failing. His main focus was not to govern the country but to raise funds for his father's ransom and to invade England; he tried to do this by raising taxes and devaluing the currency, both moves that made him intensely unpopular with his people. They were already feeling a little raw after three dramatic military defeats against the English, and it didn't take much to push them over the edge. Revolts forced Charles out of Paris. For several months, he had to ignore the Hundred Years' War in a desperate attempt to get a grip on his people. It was only in August 1358 that Charles managed to break back into Paris and regain his capital.

In 1359, King John, at that point captive in England, was desperate for freedom. He had heard that France was falling apart and that his young son was in grave danger, and he knew he had to get back at any cost—even if it meant that the English won the war. He signed a one-sided treaty that involved handing over much of French territory to the English and an almost incomprehensible ransom of four million crowns. Charles didn't have enough money to buy his father back, and he had to refuse the treaty, knowing that the consequences would be terrible. And they were.

King Edward III was an aging man by now; the teenage boy who had defied the king of France was now middle-aged and on the brink of victory. As soon as Charles rejected the treaty, Edward saw his chance. He sailed to France at the end of 1359, determined that he would be crowned king of France and seize the country now that he had already captured its king.

At first, it looked like Edward was going to succeed. Charles was back in Paris, but his health was failing; in hindsight, historians have speculated that his symptoms sounded like arsenic poisoning, so it is likely that one of his enemies was trying to kill him slowly. The army was in disarray as there was no money to arm it, and many of the nobles were still revolting against the Dauphin. Edward set his sights on Reims, traditionally the city where French kings were always crowned, and drove his army briskly toward it. There was no burning and pillaging this time—they had one objective only, and that was to make Edward the king of France.

In December 1359, Edward reached Reims and laid siege to the city. He hoped that besieging Reims would lure Charles' army into an open battlefield, where he knew that he could easily defeat the French as he had done at Crécy and Poitiers. But Charles had seen too much destruction to fall for Edward's ploy. He was going to dig into his fortified cities and hold firm as the winter fell, knowing that he had strengthened the fortifications of both Reims and Paris enough that the English could be held off.

At Reims, Edward did not launch any significant assaults. Instead, he tried to starve the city into submission even as he attempted to negotiate with it. He didn't want to raze Reims to the ground; he wanted to be crowned in it, and he was so sure of victory that he was reluctant to destroy anything more in Reims or the rest of the country because he was sure that it would soon be his to rebuild. He attempted to convince the people that he was going to be their king and that he meant nothing but good toward them, but the French remained behind their barricades and refused to hear his words. At length, after five weeks, Edward had to abandon the siege as he had run out of food for his army's horses. The army was forced to leave Reims in peace and go farther afield in search of food for the men and horses.

Edward was not about to give up, however. He swung his army toward Paris, determined to take the capital instead—if Paris fell, Reims would be his too. The Dauphin had to watch in trepidation as Edward and his army marched toward his city, but he refused to budge, staying holed up in his castle as Edward approached the suburbs, hoping to lay siege to it. It was not to be, however. While the bulk of Charles' army stayed in the fortified citadel, when Edward reached the suburbs, he was met with strong resistance by the soldiers stationed there. He was forced to retreat, realizing that the goal of Paris was a little loftier than he'd anticipated.

Instead, Edward turned toward Chartres, another major city. But he would never reach the city. A disaster was about to strike that nobody could ever have anticipated, and it would devastate the English army.

* * * *

Edward had encamped his army on an open plain, the nearby silhouette of Chartres etched against the gray sky in square black lines that spoke threateningly of the fight that was to come. He sat outside his tent, gazing out over the thousands of men and horses that surrounded him. Their armor glittered in the last of the afternoon light, and Edward couldn't help but feel a keen pang of pride. This army had achieved what many would have considered impossible, and victory was so close that he could almost taste it. Edward turned, staring around the French countryside, and smiled. Finally, he would get what was rightfully his—the crown for which he had fought so hard and for which so much blood had been shed.

A crack of thunder split the sky. Surprised, Edward looked up in time to see bitter black clouds spill across the sky, tumbling and roiling as they invaded the air. Another thunderclap made the ground tremble beneath the warrior king's boots. The horses nickered restlessly, pulling at their pickets and kicking each other in their lines as the squires ran to grab hold of them before they could break loose; knights hurried for the safety of their tents, and a restless wind began to whip at the banners above every tent, spreading them wide against the gray sky.

Then the world went white. The thunderclap was so loud that it made Edward stagger, filling his world with light and sound. Screams filled the air, and when Edward could shake the blurriness from his head, he saw a horrific sight: two of his commanders were lying motionless on the ground, smoke rising from their burnt corpses. They had been struck by lightning.

The panicked screams of men and horses filled the air as the thunder continued to snarl and pound above them. The heavens opened, and rain began to pelt down upon them, driven by the wind. The heavy droplets lashed across Edward's face and beard as he ran for cover, stinging where they landed. One of them crashed into the back of his neck, hard and icy. He paused, blinking down at the ground where the tiny missile had landed. It wasn't a raindrop. It was a massive hailstone.

The roar of hailstones pouring down upon the encampment was almost incomprehensible. They hammered on armor, ripping cloth and pounding upon the flesh of man and beast. It was too much even for the battle-trained horses. The stones were so large that they were shattering bones where they landed; horses dropped dead in the lines, men in their tents. The horses stampeded, several thousand trained destriers and fleet coursers breaking their ties and galloping across the landscape, trampling men and equipment in their mad dash for safety, falling as the hailstones struck them stone dead where they ran.

Edward could not believe his eyes. He had never seen such a storm, never even heard of it, and he knew that this freak storm was no act of mere nature. He fell to his knees and raised his face to heaven, his eyes streaming as the wind whipped his beard across his face. He screamed out to God for forgiveness, begging Him for mercy, telling Him that he saw and understood His message—that the war on France was not the Lord's will. As his men and horses died around him, King Edward III knelt and prayed in desperation.

* * * *

When the hailstorm finally abated after half an hour of carnage, Edward's army was all but destroyed. One thousand men lay dead, and six thousand dead horses littered the once peaceful landscape. It was a devastating blow, but worse still was the blow to Edward's spirit. He was convinced that the storm was an act of God made to protect the French. Clearly, he was not meant to become the king of France. Perhaps the whole war had been in vain. Either way, Edward repented. He offered to negotiate with the French.

"Black Monday," as it became known, is known even today as a freak event. The hailstorm of April 13th, 1360, held a violence that storms seldom ever have in that area. Whatever its cause, it precipitated a conference at the city of Brétigny where King Edward III signed a lasting truce known as the Treaty of Brétigny. He utterly canceled his claim to the French throne and signed over most of the territories that he and the Black Prince had gained during the war. He did gain some lands in Gascony and kept King John captive, although he lowered the ransom to three million crowns.

Even with the lowered ransom and returned lands, Prince Charles could not afford to get his father back. However, he eventually negotiated with King Edward to hand over eighty-three other hostages to be held in place for King John. King Edward accepted, and King John was released and returned to France in peace.

His freedom would not last long. One of the hostages was King John's son, Louis, who was supposed to be freed by a ransom payment within six months. When France was unable to make the payment, Louis faced a lifetime in prison. He escaped from the castle where he was being held and sailed back to France to the dismay of his father, who felt that his son's actions were dishonorable. Instead of sending Louis back, however, a heavy-hearted King John decided that it was up to him to do the honorable thing and return to England as a captive in January 1364. He died in captivity in London in April 1364, and for his faith and honor, he is known in history as King John the Good.

The first leg of the Hundred Years' War was over after twenty-three years of fighting. But the war was far from over. It had only just begun.

Section Two:
The Caroline War (1369-1389)

Chapter 6 – Charles the Wise

With his father King John II dead, the Dauphin Prince Charles became the next king of France. Before his coronation, however, he realized that there was trouble brewing on his border.

Navarre was a small kingdom between Castile and France near Gascony and was ruled over by its King Charles II. For a brief period at the beginning of the 14th century, Navarre had been a part of France; but after King Charles IV's death, it became an independent kingdom once more, and it turned upon France itself with a vengeance. Supported by the English, Navarre was disputing the possession of the dukedom of Burgundy, and King John's body was hardly cold when they launched an offensive. Their commander was a Gascon named Jean III de Grailly, Captal de Buch; he had been the one to lead the decisive charge at the Battle of Poitiers, but his luck had run out this time. The new King of France was determined not to allow Grailly to beat him twice. By pretending to retreat, he was able to fool Grailly's longbowmen into pursuing him, breaking their defensive ranks; when the Englishmen swapped their powerful bows for simple daggers, the close combat grew very heated. The Navarrese were quickly overwhelmed and suffered a decisive defeat.

Having established himself as a formidable warrior, the Dauphin returned to Reims triumphant and was crowned King Charles V. The first problem that King Charles faced was getting rid of the mercenary companies that had gone rogue after the Treaty of Brétigny of 1360. For four years, the mercenaries that had been so comfortably employed during the first stage of the Hundred Years' War found themselves without a source of income. War was all they knew, and without a war to fight, the mercenaries had no way to feed themselves. They turned to robbing and pillaging anywhere that they could, causing chaos throughout France and further crippling its failing economy. King Charles had to find some cheaper form of fighting somewhere—not attacking the mighty English directly—in order to get these mercenaries, known as the Tard-Venus, out of the country to cause havoc somewhere else.

Europe's great crusades in the Middle East had halted decades ago, but some small forays were still being made elsewhere, and this struck Charles as a useful diversion for the Tard-Venus. He tried to send them off to Hungary on a crusade, but this attempt was thwarted by France's own citizens. The people who lived in Strasbourg wanted nothing to do with having the Tard-Venus in their relatively peaceful corner of the country, and when the mercenaries approached the River Rhine, they strenuously resisted them. Angered that their king and employer's own subjects were standing against them, the Tard-Venus returned to Paris, clamoring for some other employment.

At least King Charles knew that if there was one thing that medieval Europe did not lack, it was war. Seeing that crusading would be useless, Charles set his sights on a target somewhat closer to home: Castile. Now a part of modern-day Spain, Castile was a small kingdom at the time and had been embroiled in its own civil war of succession since 1351. King Pedro of Castile—also known as Peter in the English-speaking world—had been crowned in 1350, but his illegitimate half-brother Henry of Trastámara quickly contested his rule. Pedro was unpopular with the people for being an authoritarian leader who ruled his subjects with an iron grip. While he was the rightful heir to the throne, Pedro's people didn't like him, and when Henry attempted to invade in 1351, he gained widespread support from the people. By 1365, one year after Charles had been crowned, the two brothers were fighting a grim war. Seeing a chance to not only get rid of the Tard-Venus but also to strike a blow back against the English, Charles V sent 12,000 men to Henry's aid in Castile.

This army was led by a Breton knight named Bertrand du Guesclin. Bertrand was fresh from the front of the War of the Breton Succession, where he had supported Charles of Blois. He was also a hero of the Battle of Cocherel, the recent fight between the Navarrese and the French, where he had routed the English forces commanded by Jean III de Grailly. Despite the fact that Bertrand was comparatively lowborn, his prowess on the battlefield and his skill as a military commander had already made him one of the most important military men in all of France.

Together with Henry of Trastámara, Bertrand invaded Castile in 1365. Pedro was not prepared for an invasion on such a massive scale; fortress after fortress fell to Bertrand's army, and by early 1366, Pedro had been forced out of Castile and Henry was crowned King Henry II of Castile. He was so pleased with Bertrand's service that he made him his successor, giving him the title of Count of Trastámara.

With nowhere to turn, Pedro—who had signed an alliance with England in 1362—fled to Gascony, where the Black Prince was acting as viceroy for King Edward III. He begged the Black Prince for help, but the Prince was reluctant to break the terms of the Treaty of Brétigny. Pedro ultimately managed to win him over by promising him lands in Castile, and in 1367, the Black Prince and part of his army marched on Castile. The Black Prince decided to act in his capacity as ruler of Aquitaine as opposed to prince of England, thus attempting not to break the treaty, but his attack of French troops in Castile sent a crystal-clear message to King Charles: Edward III might have repented briefly of his hunger for the French crown, but the Black Prince had no intentions of giving up on the war.

The Black Prince was indeed interested in striking back against King Charles, and he also had his eye on the Castilian navy. Its fleet of warships was much bigger and had much better ships than either his own or that of the French; he knew that he would be almost invincible on the ocean if he could gain control of that fleet. His only problem was that, with England and Gascony both plundered by war, he didn't have the money to launch an attack on a distant country. Pedro solved this problem by promising the Black Prince that he would refund him, and this played a major role in why the Black Prince agreed to march on Castile.

They arrived in La Rioja, Castile, on April 3rd, 1367, a few miles from the city of Nájera. Expecting them to come from Navarette instead, Henry had arrayed his army facing east, but the Black Prince sneaked around their flank and attacked suddenly and dramatically from the northeast. One moment a peaceful dawn was breaking; the next, Henry and Bertrand looked up to see the hill above them bristling with lances, the dramatic figure of Prince Edward in his night-black armor glittering at their head.

Despite the fact that Henry's army only numbered about half that of Pedro and the Black Prince, he and Bertrand courageously faced the might of the Gascons, but it was all in vain. Seeing that they could never win, many of Henry's soldiers defected to Pedro's side in the middle of the battle; hard-pressed on every side, the last loyal few fought to the very death. More than half of Henry's army was killed. Henry himself managed to flee across the Pyrenees and sought refuge in France, but Bertrand was captured and ransomed by the Black Prince.

Yet it was not a victory for the English in the end: it was a victory for Pedro. In a deceitful move that would eventually alienate him from most of Europe, Pedro failed to pay any of his debts to the Black Prince, who was forced to return to Gascony in 1368 with empty hands and an army that had been utterly ravaged by Spanish illnesses for which they had no immunity. In a desperate attempt to pay back the debts the Black Prince himself had incurred in order to support Pedro, he heavily taxed Gascony.

The Black Prince's Gascon subjects were already restless before the tax. Many of the Black Prince's countrymen had moved to Gascony with him, and he had given them positions of power, making the native Gascons feel oppressed. The taxes only made matters worse. One such disgruntled minor nobleman was Arnaud-Amanieu VIII, Lord of Albret. While he had been part of the campaign against Henry, Albret had expected to be handsomely compensated for his trouble, not to be taxed so harshly after it. He refused to pay the taxes and appealed to Charles V for support. The king, who was delighted to see his enemy in trouble, issued a summons to bring Albret and the Black Prince to Paris for a hearing. Enraged, the Black Prince responded that the only way he would be going to Paris would be with an army. It was not quite a declaration of war, but it was enough to incense King Charles. Knowing his enemy was financially crippled, he forfeited the English lands in France, and the Black Prince—who was ailing from some illness he had picked up in Castile, potentially even poison itself—found himself trying to control a duchy that had revolted against him and joined his enemy.

Even Castile was no longer a friend to Prince Edward. Encouraged by the fact that the formidable Black Prince had returned to Gascony and was unlikely to ever extend aid to Pedro again, Henry attacked Castile again in 1369 and restored himself to power, murdering his half-brother.

The Castilian Civil War was over. But the Hundred Years' War was back in full swing.

Chapter 7 – The Death of John Chandos

Illustration III: The Abbey Church of Saint-Savin, which is a UNESCO World Heritage Site today

Sir John Chandos was an old man by medieval standards. At about fifty-five, he had seen more than his fair share of war, and he was tiring of the war with the French that had begun when he was just a young man of seventeen. He had been one of the knights that reconnoitered the tethered ships on that misty morning before the Battle of Sluys; he, too, had been at the Battle of Crécy and was instrumental in drawing up the strategy that had made the battle such a magnificent success. He had fought at Najera, as well, following the black armor of Prince Edward across the continent as he sought to prove his chivalry and courage, just as any good knight of his era would.

He was a courageous knight, but more than that, he was an intellectual. While it was King Edward and his son that had executed the plans that produced brilliant victories at both Crécy and Poitiers, Sir John had been the mastermind behind them. He was a most devoted friend of the Black Prince, becoming to England what Bertrand du Guesclin was to France. His strength as a strategist, commander, and diplomat won him the title of constable of Gascony in 1362.

While the Hundred Years' War was supposedly at a truce at the time, Sir John had no lack of battles in which to further prove himself. It was Sir John that led the last battle of the War of the Breton Succession, that struggle between French-backed Charles of Blois and English favorite John of Montfort that had been raging for years. At the Battle of Auray in September 1364, Sir John Chandos and John of Montfort besieged the fortress of Auray, beating Charles of Blois and Bertrand du Guesclin in a heated battle that killed Charles of Blois and effectively put an end to the War of the Breton Succession. John of Montfort was made Duke of Brittany, and Sir John returned to Gascony a well-proven hero and was highly acclaimed in his position as constable of Gascony.

Shortly afterward, however, he clashed with the king about the strict taxation that the Black Prince was imposing on the people and decided to retire from his military and administrative career. Sir John headed to his property in Normandy in a bid to live out the rest of his days in peace.

But it was not to be. By late 1369, Gascony was in revolt, and the Black Prince was struggling to control the territory he already had—never mind that which he hoped to gain from France. Now in his fifties, Sir John was forced to return to war when King Edward III recalled him, seeing that the English were going to need every man they could get if they could even vaguely hope to bring France back under control.

Sir John was sent to Poitiers, the same place where he had helped to defeat the French in the battle that had seen King John the Good captured. But John the Good was dead, and his vengeful son King Charles V was determined to take back what his father had lost. As winter settled upon the French landscape, King Charles began to tighten the noose around the English. Only a few miles away from Poitiers, two of his lords occupied small castles, their forces slowly creeping ever nearer.

Sir John watched this with trepidation. He knew that he didn't have the resources that he'd once used in the previous battles where he had proven himself so successful; the Castilian campaign had financially crippled the Black Prince, and English troops were spread thinly across a country that was thoroughly in revolt. Still, he decided it was worth his while to attempt to retake Saint-Savin, a large abbey near Poitiers that was under the control of Frenchman Louis de Saint Julien Trimouille, lord of Lusignan.

Under cover of darkness, Sir John's men crept forward across the wintry landscape, heading for the abbey. Its long, straight roof, topped at one end with a sharp tower that stabbed between the stars, was cut out as a black silhouette against the silver night. Frost crunched beneath the feet of Sir John's men as they fixed their eyes on the golden squares that the abbey's windows lit up in the night. The torchlight was in rippling reflection in the waters of the Seine below, on whose very bank the abbey was built.

Quietly, Sir John and his knights made their way toward the abbey. Then, the sound of horses. Sir John brought his men sharply to a halt and listened. Frenchmen! They had been discovered! In a hushed panic, Sir John hustled his men back toward Poitiers in an organized retreat toward the Vienne River. He planned to cross the bridge at Lussac, hoping that they could slip back to Poitiers without French discovery. He knew that the English would be horribly outnumbered—and, worse still, that they had left Poitiers itself barely defended.

Galloping through the night, the French riders had no idea that the English were planning to attack Saint-Savin at all. Despite what Sir John thought, the French didn't even know that he and his men were in the area. Their ride was simply to check if there were any Englishmen in the area, and it took them straight across the bridge at Lussac.

It was on the bridge that they met. Hooves and feet rang on the stone surface of the high bridge as the two armies plunged across the Vienne to meet one another in a violent skirmish. Swords clashed, screams resounding through the winter night. Sir John, as always, was at the front of his army, rushing forward to meet the enemy. But as he charged, his boot caught on the hem of his long cloak. The stone bridge was slick with frost, and before a French hand could be raised against him, Sir John slipped and fell heavily to the ground.

Seeing his chance, a French squire named James de Saint-Martin rushed upon the fallen commander. Stabbing forward with his lance, James struck Sir John solidly in the face, laying his cheek open and piercing his skull with the tip of the lance. Blood burst out onto stone and frost, and Sir John's uncle Edward Twyford charged forth to his rescue. Twyford's own squire rushed upon James and quickly avenged Sir John with two blows of his sword, slicing James's legs open—wounds that would eventually lead to James' death a few days later.

Despite Twyford's valiant attempts to save both the Englishmen and Sir John, it was for naught. The English were scattered, fleeing back toward the nearest English stronghold, Morthemer. Sweeping across the landscape, the French had obtained their first foothold needed for retaking Poitiers, undoing what had been done at that decisive English victory of 1356.

Sir John himself was still alive, if only barely. Groaning and barely able to move or speak, he was gently lifted onto a shield and carried on the shoulders of his men to Morthemer. Despite their best efforts to save him, Sir John's wounds were too grievous. He died about twenty-four hours later on the last night of 1369.

* * * *

The Black Prince and the King of England both bitterly mourned Sir John's passing. He had been one of England's best commanders, a key player in its early victories during the Hundred Years' War. His admirers were many and included even his archenemy, Bertrand du Guesclin. King Charles himself regretted Sir John's death, too, believing that if he had been captured instead of killed, he might have helped to bring peace between England and France at last. Historians on both sides speculate that if Sir John had not been killed so prematurely, he might have ended the Hundred Years' War one way or another.

But Sir John was dead, and nobody wanted peace. The English were desperate to hold on to the lands they still had; the French were equally desperate to strike back at the nation that had done them so much damage. Piece by piece, King Charles began to claw back the lands that had belonged to his late father.

Land was not the only thing that King Charles was interested in reclaiming. While John of Montfort now ruled Brittany and supported the English, the French had a strong ally in the form of King Henry of Castile. While Castile's land forces were not much compared to the might of the French cavalry, their naval fleet was a force to be reckoned with, and King Charles soon set his sights on regaining something that he hadn't had since the Battle of Sluys:

control over the English Channel. If he could stop English reinforcements from reaching France at Calais, perhaps he could stop the war in its tracks.

Chapter 8 – A French Victory

England was in trouble.

With Sir John Chandos dead and the Black Prince too sick to leave his castle, the heroes of Poitiers were all but gone. King Edward III himself was an aged man by this point, a far cry from the stubborn teenager who had first started the war; he was too old to lead any form of attack. England found itself without money to put together a real army and without seasoned commanders to lead it.

The only war hero that remained on the English side was Jean III de Grailly, Captal de Buch. He, too, had fought at the English victories in Poitiers and Najera. Now, with Sir John Chandos gone, Grailly was made Constable of Aquitaine (Gascony). He soon learned of a new commander who had barely won his spurs: twenty-five-year-old John Hastings, 2nd Earl of Pembroke. Pembroke had served with the Black Prince before the latter grew too sick to fight anymore; on his return to England, he had been made Lieutenant of Aquitaine.

It was the summer of 1372. Sir John Chandos had been dead for two years, the Black Prince and King Edward were both in England,

and Grailly was starting to feel like he was trying to single-handedly withstand the growing strength of the French. He was glad to hear the news that the Earl of Pembroke was on his way to France, sailing to the relief of Gascony—at least Grailly hoped.

Pembroke sailed from Plymouth with a small fleet of about twenty ships (although records of exactly how many ships he had differ), most of them small, protected by only three large warships. His idea was to raise an army of men in Gascony itself, and so he carried only a handful of soldiers, with one ship being dedicated solely to carrying a gigantic amount of silver coin with which he intended to pay his new army. He had instructions to amass over three thousand men with which to attack the French. But his plans all had to change when he heard that the French had besieged La Rochelle. The city and fortress were located on the Bay of Biscay in Gascony, Pembroke's intended destination, and its situation was dire by the time he drew near. Bertrand du Guesclin had laid siege to the city; his forces were large, and he was aided by a large fleet from the legendary Castilian navy. Swift galleys from the unmatched Castile navy waited in the bay, protecting the town from reinforcements that would arrive by sea.

Grailly had already attempted to relieve La Rochelle by a land-based attack. It was a terrible failure; he accidentally encountered a Welsh mercenary serving the French who successfully captured Grailly and shipped him off to Paris, where he would be imprisoned for the rest of his life. Hope was running out for La Rochelle.

Even though Pembroke knew that his fleet was pitiable in comparison with the larger and better-armed force of the Castilians, he also knew that he had to do something to try to save the town. He changed his course toward the doomed city and sailed forth with little more than hope and courage to spur his men onward.

On June 21st, 1372, the beleaguered citizens of La Rochelle first spotted the sleek form of an English warship on the shimmering blue expanse of the bay. The bows of the English ships and transports bristled with the curved forms of longbows, a brave and brilliant sight that brought hope to La Rochelle. What they didn't know was that Pembroke had about fifty ships compared to Castile's fleet of a little more than twenty ships, all of them purposed for war instead of transport. These were Castilian galleys, vastly superior vessels to the lumbering English cogs that were still in use. The galleys were fast and agile and could maneuver easily even in fairly shallow waters, while the cogs sat low in the water and needed more space to turn.

Still, Pembroke had to try. He bravely sailed straight for the Castilians, and the galleys surged forward to meet him, sure of their victory. As the longbowmen launched their arrows at the Castilian ships, they were answered with a deafening crack, followed by the thin whine of a cannonball sailing through the air. With a splintering thud, it punched into the English ships, ripping men and ships apart. The Castilians had cannons, and they knew exactly how to use them.

Despite the superior numbers and weapons of the Castilians, the English refused to back down. They put up a strenuous resistance, despite the fact that their ships were sinking all around them. A fierce battle ensued for several hours as the English did their best to keep the Castilians at bay. When the tide began to rise, the exhausted fleets broke apart, the English fleeing toward the open sea. Night was falling, and the Castilians opted to return to the bay to anchor for the night instead of pursuing their opponents.

While the English lay at anchor a little way off the shore, some of La Rochelle's residents scraped together their resolve and decided to come to the aid of their would-be rescuers. Three knights and four barges set sail at daybreak, heading out of the bay and toward the rest of the English fleet. They hoped to sneak past the Castilians and join their allies; instead, they only seemed to rouse the sleeping monster of their enemy. Springing into action, the swift Castilian galleys charged across the water. The English ships all attempted to face them, but the low tide was their downfall; some of the ships had run aground, and the galleys were flying through the shallow water, surrounding the English in minutes.

Oil sprayed from the Castilian ships, launched by the sailors so that it splattered on the deck and rigging of an English ship. Before the ship's commanders could react, there was the twang of a bowstring from one of the galleys, and an arrow launched into the air, an oil-soaked cloth wrapped around its head and set alight so that the bright flame roared and flickered as the arrow flew toward the English ship. With a slap, the arrow lodged itself in the oil-soaked wood. There was a roar of flame, and the entire ship was engulfed in blazing fire. Thick, black smoke rose from the burning ship as its men screamed, their clothes alight, and plunged into the water.

England was still fighting, but it had already been defeated. The fight had been almost too easy for the brilliant Castilians. One by one, the ships were grappled—where grappling hooks were thrown onto their decks to allow the Castilians to board them—and their soldiers either killed or taken prisoner. Pembroke was one of those who ended up as a prisoner of Castile.

As for the English fleet, it was utterly and completely lost. All of the ships were either sunk or captured and triumphantly carried off to Castile once more. The twelve thousand British pounds' worth of silver coins that Pembroke had brought to Gascony in the hope of paying his soldiers were all lost, falling into the hands of the Castilians.

La Rochelle itself would hold out courageously for more than two months. Finally, on September 7th, the city could not maintain the siege anymore. It fell to du Guesclin and became yet another of his victories.

With the Black Prince and King Edward both stuck in England, Sir John Chandos dead, Jean III de Grailly and the Earl of Pembroke both captured, all seemed utterly lost for England. But there was going to be one more attempt to get Gascony back. And it would be made by a wealthy English prince named John of Gaunt.

Chapter 9 – The Great Chevauchée

Illustration IV: John of Gaunt

Their confidence bolstered by the victory at La Rochelle, the combined navies of France and Castile decided to make a bold move. The Isle of Wight, then an English territory, was just across the English Channel from France, and it was a tempting target. In

1373, the combined fleet set sail for the little island with just one aim: to take and destroy. The fleet bore down upon the island in an unstoppable wave, and with the English army mostly crippled, they found it poorly guarded. With little resistance, the Isle of Wight was thoroughly sacked, and much of it burned to the ground.

The Frenchmen and their allies returned triumphantly to France, believing that the war on England was practically over. But this was far from the truth. The Black Prince might have been languishing back in England, only a few years from his young deathbed, but one of his brothers wasn't done with the war.

* * * *

John of Gaunt was the fourth son of King Edward III and his wife, Philippa of Hainault. A tall, strong man, he was similar to his sickly brother in many ways and had always seemed to find himself in the Black Prince's shadow. He had campaigned with him in both France and Castile, but when he was in command of a small army himself, he had been met mostly with stalemates. After the Siege of Limoges in 1370, the Black Prince made him Lieutenant of Aquitaine and then returned to England, but John found himself trying to do little except cling on to the scraps of land that was still in English possession. Utterly frustrated by his failures and England's apparently imminent defeat, John resigned and returned to England.

Still, he wasn't done with trying to gain the upper hand over France, and he also wasn't done trying to live up to his big brother. He knew that England would not be able to beat France in a pitched battle at that point, but there was one more tactic he could use—a tactic that had been successfully used by the Black Prince, as well. A chevauchée. A recent outbreak of the Black Death in 1369 had left both the French and English armies somewhat decreased, but John was still able to scrape together a force of nine thousand men and thirty thousand horses. It was enough to do heavy damage to France—enough to destroy plenty of villages and obtain plenty of plunder. Perhaps, with France economically wounded and some extra loot for England, it would be enough for John to bring glory to his own name and to restart England's offensive. He hoped it could even be enough to turn the tables on France.

Financial trouble and the plague had been stifling John's attempts to plan the chevauchée for three years. But finally, in August 1373, the great march began. A sea of men and horses set forth from Calais, the force of thirty thousand sets of iron-rimmed hooves pounding the earth, causing the entire landscape to tremble. It would have been a sight both magnificent and terrifying: a great swarm of armored horses, mounted by knights whose steel armor flashed in the summer sun, their ranks ablaze with banners and emblazoned shields, their lances stabbing up into the air. John set his sights on Gascony, which was all the way across France. To reach it, his men would have to cross hundreds of miles of enemy territory, burning every village they came across and carrying their loot with them. They could only hope that the French would avoid battle.

Traveling this kind of distance with such a large amount of living creatures—almost forty thousand all told, including the horses—was no mean feat during this time. While provisions for the men could be loaded into saddlebags, the horses were far more complicated to care for. The average human only consumes about five and a half pounds of food every day; the average horse, sixteen pounds or more. There was no way that enough food for the horses could be carried with them, so they were forced to stop and allow the horses to graze—and the sheer amount of space needed to graze thirty thousand horses every day was mind-boggling. Added to this, each horse would need about ten gallons of water every day, meaning that three hundred thousand gallons of water were consumed by the horses alone.

To feed the giant cavalry, the army was forced to forage, sending out small parties of riders to search for good grazing and a water source. And it was here that France would strike. King Charles was well aware of the chevauchée that was plundering its way across his country, and he did not plan to allow it to continue unchecked. While France had still not defeated England in a major land battle yet, making Charles reluctant to face the army head-on, he knew that if he shadowed it closely and harried its edges, he would wear it down eventually. His tactic worked. The small groups of riders that had gone out to forage, scout, or plunder were faced with swift but devastating attacks from the French. There was no major battle, but the French never once left the side of the English force, continually harassing it, always ready to wear it down.

Initially, the chevauchée was fairly successful, meeting with little resistance as it moved through France's northern provinces. But things took a sharp turn for the worse as they approached Burgundy. The French army that had been following them closely started to press them harder, forcing the English up against the Allier River. They escaped pitched battle but only just; they were forced over the bridge at Moulins in such haste that all of their baggage and loot was lost.

It was November by this point, and the kind summer that had made the advancing army such a splendid sight as they left Calais was over. Instead, winter was settling upon the Limousin Plateau, and it promised to be harsh. Frost started to ravage the landscape, making the nights unbearably cold for men whose bodies and spirits were already suffering after months of travel and fighting. Worse, the frost was killing off the abundant grazing that the army's horses had so strongly depended on. One by one, men and horses started to freeze and starve to death. As the horses died in the thousands, the men found themselves without mounts, forced to march on foot alongside the rest of the army. This was almost impossible to do in full armor and weaponry, considering that a knight's suit of armor alone weighed as much as fifty-five pounds. The army's attention had now turned from plundering to simply surviving the trek to

Gascony. The dismounted knights had no thought for battle—they simply wanted to make it out of enemy territory as quickly as possible. They abandoned their armor where it lay and marched onward, leaving littering heaps of expensive steel everywhere that the army passed.

France still avoided a battle, but as more and more of the army began to straggle behind, they picked off small groups as they went. John's men had nothing left to fight the Frenchmen with. He abandoned all hope of plundering France further and took the most careful route he could to Gascony, avoiding any fortified cities, aiming only to get his men off the plateau alive.

At the beginning of December, four months after leaving Calais, they finally got to Gascony. The army was a poor shadow of the majestic force that had started the chevauchée. They had no loot; they barely had any armor or weapons left on their backs, stumbling across to Bordeaux half-destroyed. Of the thirty thousand horses that had left Calais, only fifteen thousand entered Bordeaux, and they were sickly, skinny creatures with all the fight taken out of them. The men, too, had sunken cheeks and hollow eyes. John of Gaunt was named for the place where he had been born—Ghent—but gaunt was his appearance, too, as he swayed into Bordeaux atop a horse whose ribs stood out like hoops beneath a thinned and scruffy coat. The Great Chevauchée had been a courageous feat, but it had also been a complete failure. It plundered England's resources more than it did France's, and while some of John's contemporaries would admire him for the courage of a four-month march in such challenging conditions, the people back in England resented him for his failure.

The English peasants had long been paying the price for their king's hope to claim France for himself. Resentment was brewing, and John's failure was another straw on the back of a camel who was not about to break—it was about to turn red-eyed and feral. Trouble was brewing on John's home turf. And it would cost him dearly.

Chapter 10 – Two Boy Kings

The end of John of Gaunt's Great Chevauchée marked the end of major hostilities in France for the next few years. However, the Franco-Castilian fleet that had so successfully sacked the Isle of Wight was not done with exacting its vengeance for all the harm that England had done both to the French Crown and to Henry of Castile.

In 1377, the French and the Castilians launched a series of major raids that would cripple some of England's most important port towns. Sailing their swift galleys effortlessly across the English Channel, they started to terrorize city after English city, sacking and burning some of the country's most important ports: Hastings, Plymouth, Portsmouth, Rye.

These port towns found themselves largely undefended against the invaders from France—many of whom sailed from La Rochelle itself—because England was about to be plunged into a period of turmoil. Edward the Black Prince, the hero of the war, was on his deathbed.

At the age of forty-five, the Black Prince was no longer a young man. He had been sick—very sick—ever since the campaign in

Castile during the late 1360s. While some historians have speculated that the Black Prince may have fallen sick due to poisoning by Pedro the Cruel, who wanted to avoid paying the debts he had incurred when he begged for England's help in the Castilian Civil War, it is more likely that he contracted some disease for which he had no immunity. Whatever caused his illness, it lingered for many years. The Black Prince had been an invalid ever since his return to Aquitaine. He finally gave up on fighting the war after the Siege of Limoges in 1370, returning to England in 1371. By the summer of 1376, he had been sick for nearly ten years.

It felt to the prince like an inglorious disgrace that he would die so slowly, so painfully, and so ignominiously after his many feats in the war. He had been living by the sword ever since he was a boy; it seemed a terrible thing to him that he would be denied the honor of dying by it. Even the disabled King of Bohemia, John the Blind, had been able to strike one last blow in his age and infirmity. But not the Black Prince, the hero of England. He died slowly and in agony, finally dying on June 8th, 1376. He had been the heir to the throne for decades, but he would never sit upon it.

King Edward III himself—the man who had started the war in the first place—was also not far from his own grave. Like his son, he had been a warrior all his life, fighting both in the Hundred Years' War and with Scotland; like his son, he also would not die in battle. In his age and infirmity, the king had become little more than a slave to his power-grabbing mistress, Alice Perrers, who corrupted the entire government. Since 1374, he had not had much of a role in governing his country, with John of Gaunt instead acting as an unofficial regent for the aging king.

The Black Prince had only been dead for a year when his father followed. Having been sick for several months, King Edward had just begun to recover from an abscess when he died suddenly of a stroke on June 21st, 1377. He had been king of England for fifty years.

Perhaps John of Gaunt hoped that he would become king of England now. He had, after all, been governing the country for several years, and he was the only real military commander that England had left. But it was not to be. The new king, Richard II, was crowned on July 16th, 1377. He was the eldest surviving son of the Black Prince, and he was only ten years old.

Richard had been born in Bordeaux, Aquitaine in 1367 during his father's Castilian campaign. Because he was only a child at the time of his coronation, Richard would normally have been appointed a regent—a group of advisers who would effectively reign in his stead, normally consisting of his uncles. However, John of Gaunt's corrupt political decisions had made him wildly unpopular with both the commoners and the nobility. John was one of the richest men in the country; he owned land across England and wasn't afraid to show how lucrative his patrimony had made him, living in the lap of luxury—a fact that chafed the common people who often lived in disease and squalor. This, coupled with his reinstatement of the hated Alice Perrers and autocratic attitude, caused resentment among the nobility. It was ultimately decided to allow Richard to reign himself, albeit aided by some councils that did not include John of Gaunt.

Despite these measures, it was immediately evident that Richard was well under the influence of his uncle. John had gotten used to power when he was in charge during King Edward's old age, and he was not about to let go of any of it.

While this was going on in England, France itself was not experiencing a time of stability either. King Charles V of France was sick. While he had succeeded in winning back almost all of the lands that France had lost in the Treaty of Brétigny, he had no intentions of trying to win back Calais or Gascony. Instead, he wanted peace. Negotiations with the English had been unfruitful, however, and the two countries had achieved only a few uneasy truces when King Charles developed an abscess on his arm. He was only forty-two years old, but it was evident to the king that if the abscess dried up instead of bursting, he was going to die. With only the most primitive medicine available in the medieval era, there was little that his physicians could do for him. The abscess did indeed dry up, and King Charles died on September 16th, 1380.

Despite the fact that King Charles V had only been twelve years old when he married Jeanne de Bourbon and had produced his first child at the age of nineteen, he did not have an adult heir. His first two sons had only survived a few years; it was only in 1368 that he would produce a son that would survive to adulthood. This boy was only eleven years old when his father died, but he was promptly crowned King Charles VI of France.

With two boy kings upon the thrones of the warring nations, it was hoped that peace would come between them. But this war would span for generations. First, though, Richard II would face his first great challenge on his home turf: the Peasants' Revolt.

* * * *

Richard was fourteen years old, and most of his kingly decisions were not being made by himself but by John of Gaunt. John had been unpopular with the peasants even before the failure of his raid on France; he continued to make corrupt decisions that made him still more unpopular, and the peasants started to tell stories that questioned his relation to the late King Edward III. This enraged him. John had little regard for the poor people who worked in the fields of his country; as serfs, they were little more than slaves, forced laborers who had no say in their work. John saw them as practically cattle, and he treated them as such.

Even though the serfs engaged in forced labor, they were still allowed to own possessions, and as such, they were expected to pay taxes as well. The most hated tax of all was known as the poll tax. Unlike the hearth tax, which was levied per household—and thus supposedly per family—the poll tax was levied per adult and was usually almost unaffordable for the penniless peasants of that era. Worse, peasants and nobility were asked to pay exactly the same tax regardless of their income. Thus, what was easy for the nobility to pay was cripplingly expensive for the lower classes.

The poll tax was usually only used during times of necessity, which only made matters worse for the peasants. John of Gaunt, after more or less taking over the government around 1375, immediately saw it as a solution to his financial problems. He levied his first poll tax in 1377, then again in 1379. Just as the serfs were starting to recover from this double blow, John did it once again, instituting a poll tax in 1381.

The peasants had had enough. They knew they had to do something or face starving their own families in order to pay the tax, which was generally enforced by imprisonment or other harsh penalties. The opinions of a peasant, who was usually illiterate and utterly uneducated, were not considered to be valid. They knew that words would achieve nothing. Instead, they had to rebel against the hated administration and the cruel fist of John of Gaunt.

In May 1381, the rebellion started in earnest in Brentwood, Essex. A royal official was trying to collect some of the unpaid poll taxes in the town when the peasants rose up against him. Wielding agricultural tools and a handful of weapons, artisans, serfs, and village officials alike took to the streets, attacking the tax collectors, setting fire to the village records, and throwing open the doors of the gaols (jails) to set free those who had failed to pay the unobtainable sum of the taxes.

The revolt quickly spread throughout Essex, continuing to Kent and then onward to London. They reached the capital of England on June 13th, where they set their sights on a target related to the man they hated more than anyone else: John of Gaunt. His Savoy Palace was a gorgeous and gaudy residence containing enough gold and silver to pay the poll tax of hundreds—if not thousands—of peasants. They tore the place to the ground. Declining to steal a single item, the peasants instead destroyed it all. They crushed the jewels, set fire to the luxurious furnishings upon which John rested while they slept on straw and cold earth, and threw what they couldn't destroy into the murky waters of the Thames. John happened not to be in the palace at the time, or it is likely they would have done their utmost to destroy him, too; he was foremost upon the list of people that the peasants demanded Richard hand over to them for execution.

After a night of chaos, with building after building being burned to the ground, Richard knew that he had to do something. He would have to negotiate with the peasants.

It could not have been an easy task for a fourteen-year-old king. Never could the crown have weighed more heavily on his youthful head than on that day as he walked warily to a district of East London known as Mile End. He only had a tiny handful of men with him for protection; against the angry masses of the peasants, they did not seem like much. But Richard went, and he heard out the complaints and demands of the peasants. At first, he agreed to go along with many of their requests. Returning to one of his royal houses—the Tower of London being by this time taken by the rebels—Richard started to put together charters that would abolish the very idea of serfdom itself.

However, only two days later, news reached the king that the ringleader of the peasants was dead. Wat Tyler had been the instigator and leader of much of the rebellion, and once he was gone, the peasants found themselves disunited and uncertain. Richard sent armies out to suppress what was left of the rebellion. By the end of June, order was being more or less restored, with the serfs returning to forced labor. All that they had really achieved was to avoid paying the poll tax.

Richard had succeeded in clinging to power despite his youth. But there were bigger challenges coming than a mere group of peasants staging a failed rebellion. Richard had enemies in many places, and one of them was the twelve-year-old King Charles VI of France. Yet another was closer to home. Much closer.

Chapter 11 – Madness and Deposition

Hostilities between France and England had all but ceased at this point. There had only been one short raid on France again since John of Gaunt's failed chevauchée: a brief and failed expedition led by Richard's uncle, Thomas of Woodstock, which took place in 1380.

    The two young kings of France and England were too busy trying to manage their own countries to wage war on one another. France was experiencing revolts of its own in 1382, its boy king struggling to maintain a grip on restless peasants who were tired of decades of taxation in order to fund a war that had brought them nothing but grief. This was despite the fact that King Charles V had done his best to replenish the coffers that had found themselves so plundered by the war: those same coffers had been brutally emptied by the corrupt group of King Charles VI's uncles who had been in charge of the regency until the young king was able to take his throne. Charles VI felt he had no choice but to heavily tax the peasants, and they rebelled against it, refusing to pay the taxes and rising up in two minor rebellions.

To make matters worse, Bertrand du Guesclin had died in the same year as King Charles V. France found itself without leadership except for a corrupt regency and a boy king, and within a few years, all the work that Charles V had done in order to build a victory for France had been undone. The country was in no position to be fighting wars.

As the early 1380s wore on and Richard grew into a young man, it became evident that he had little ambition for the French crown. He made only two half-hearted attempts to reignite the stalling war; a brief crusade by the Bishop of Norwich, followed by Richard's personal expedition into Scotland—still one of France's major allies—both failed in rapid succession, the first in 1383 and the other in 1385. After this, Richard appeared to lose all interest in the war.

This angered many of Richard's advisers. He was faced with his first royal crisis as early as 1386 when a group of lords started to push back against him. This included John of Gaunt—who was angered by Richard's military failures, which so abysmally echoed his own—and his son, Henry of Bolingbroke, then Earl of Derby. While Richard was able to scrape together something resembling peace in a couple of years, the damage had been done—his nobility disrespected him, and his commoners distrusted him due to his failure to follow up on his promises of abolishing serfdom. The king was on dangerous footing.

One thing that the group of lords, known as the Lords Appellant, did succeed in doing during their uprising against Richard and his cronies was an attempt to reignite the war in France. However, with the royal coffers thoroughly emptied by a corrupt king (Richard's favoritism having led him to spoil some select courtiers rather than truly invest in his country), the attempt never got off the ground. By 1389, the war had come to something of a stalemate, with both countries effectively defeated by their own people. On July 18th, 1389, the two kings signed the Truce of Leulinghem. The truce allowed Richard to reclaim all the lands in Gascony that had recently been lost in the war, as well as to maintain the fortress at Calais; however, he still had to pay homage to King Charles VI, and there was now no question that his claim to the French throne was utterly nullified.

Peace descended upon the nations, bringing an end to the Caroline phase of the war. Even the proxy wars began to die down throughout Europe. Still, neither country experienced real peace. With Richard perpetually squabbling with his court, England's people found themselves in a period of instability. France, on the other hand, had recently been officially taken over by its young King Charles VI. He was a well-educated young man who pushed his corrupt uncles out of the court and replaced them with advisers of his own, and perhaps the people of France believed that things were looking up for them.

They were, until history—and their lives—would take a turn that nobody could have expected. King Charles the Beloved was about to earn a new title: the Mad.

* * * *

In 1392, a hot-tempered aristocrat named Pierre de Craon, in a fit of rage, attempted to murder one of King Charles' trusted friends and advisers, a man named Olivier de Clisson. He failed to kill Clisson, and he realized at once that he had made a terrible mistake. Fleeing to Brittany, Craon hoped to escape the wrath of the king.

Angered by this blatant attempt on Clisson's life, King Charles at once summoned an army. On July 1st, 1392, he set off through the summer countryside of sunny France, out for Craon's blood. His knights sensed that something was amiss before they even started their march. Charles was fevered, frenzied almost; his speech was garbled, his zeal to find and kill Craon so severe that it was nearly delusional. The knights knew better than to criticize their king though. They followed him meekly through the country, keeping their heads down as he bellowed at them to move faster, faster, because the traitor was getting away.

The march was long, the army dragging its feet more and more as the men started to wonder why their king was behaving so strangely. The August sun was beating down on the ranks of men and horses when a strange cry tore through the forest. The knights sprang to attention, then relaxed as a ragged, barefoot tramp rushed through the woods. They were so surprised at his appearance that they failed to stop him rushing straight up to the king. Seizing the bridle of Charles' mount, he cried out, "Ride no further, noble King!"

Charles simply sat and listened, wide eyes burning in a fever-red face, as the man urged him to turn back and warned him of treachery. He was still mid-scream when the knights came to their senses and drove him off, yet the man continued to follow the army at a safe distance, shouting his chilling warning.

The knights dismissed him as crazy. But Charles could not forget the man's words. He'd been born into a continent ablaze with war, grown up in a court that was filled with greed and personal ambition that would not shy from assassinating an opponent. Paranoia began to seep into his bruised psyche. He was as tense as a drawn bowstring, and the smallest thing could release the arrow.

The moment came somewhere near noon. The king was accompanied by several pages—boys between the ages of seven and fourteen, usually in training to become knights—who were tasked with carrying his extra armor and weaponry. They had been marching for weeks, sitting on plump sumpter ponies who plodded along without breaking rhythm, and the sun was warm and kind on their shoulders. Lulled to sleep, one of the pages dropped the king's lance. It tumbled from his hands and crashed onto a helmet—borne by another page—with a deafening clang.

The sound ignited King Charles. Spinning around in the saddle, he whipped out his sword, the length of its gleaming blade flashing razor-edged in the sun. "Forward against the traitors!" he cried out, and, before anyone could stop him, he fell upon his own knights. The man they'd sworn to serve and protect was suddenly out to kill them, his blade butchering his own army.

It took several men to disarm Charles and wrestle him to the ground, pinning him down and forcing him to surrender, although no one dared harm him. Charles struggled at first but then suddenly went limp in the grip of his men. He had fallen into a coma.

The hunt for Craon was abandoned; King Charles was bound and returned to Paris, but when he awoke from his sleep, he appeared to be his usual self once more. Yet it would not remain that way. King Charles had gone officially insane. When he was lucid, he appeared to be a good leader, wise and intelligent, but these moments did not last. In his madness, he was a nightmare. Running naked through the castle grounds, refusing to eat or bathe, failing to recognize his own wife, and even spending several months believing that he was made entirely of glass and would shatter if touched—a delusion that was later identified as strangely common in the late Middle Ages—were all symptoms of Charles's mental illness. Today, scholars have speculated that these periods of psychosis could have been caused by schizophrenia or bipolar disorder. In his time, he was simply known as mad.

Charles' reign was immediately taken over by a regency, once again comprised of his corrupt uncles. His brother, Louis I, Duke of Orléans, who had assisted Charles in gaining control in the first place, attempted to oust the uncles. France's government dissolved into absolute chaos.

England was not faring much better. In 1399, King Richard II was deposed. The man responsible for the deposition was none other than Henry of Bolingbroke, the son of John of Gaunt. Henry had spent too much time watching his father spend his life playing second fiddle; he did not plan to do the same. He had been exiled in Paris during a time when Louis was in charge of the regency. The latter was interested in restarting the war, and knowing that Richard was interested in peace, he allowed Henry to return to England in the hopes that the war would flare up again.

Henry unceremoniously removed Richard from his post on October 1st, 1399, backed up by many of London's politicians who had grown tired of Richard's favoritism. He was crowned King Henry IV while Richard, kept in imprisonment, was allowed to starve slowly to death—as so many of the peasants had underneath the harsh poll tax.

Section Three:
The Lancastrian War
(1415-1453)

Chapter 12 – Besieging Harfleur

Despite the hopes of Louis of Orléans, current regent of France, the new King of England did not renew the war on France. Henry IV's hands were much too busy dealing with domestic troubles, the first being a Welsh uprising in 1400, only a few months after he was crowned.

While the threat of a French invasion was present, it never came to pass, potentially because of the complications of dealing with King Charles the Mad. His fits of madness were growing increasingly frequent as he aged to the point where his men had to wall up some of the corridors of his castle so that he couldn't wander too far and hurt himself. Occasionally he still grew violent and dangerous, so much so that he sometimes had to be restrained to prevent him from once again murdering one of his own knights. So, the fragile peace held, although pirates and privateers marauded the English Channel from both sides.

It is possible that Henry IV might have attacked France again once the uprisings had been crushed, but he never had the chance. He was still trying to stop the Percy Rebellion in Northumberland when he suffered a mysterious attack of illness that involved a loss of consciousness, possibly even a seizure, during 1405. It was not the last attack of its kind, although its exact cause is still unknown to historians; it may have been epilepsy or have had cardiovascular origins. He suffered similar episodes about once or twice a year for the rest of his life, as well as having a skin disease so severe that it forced him to withdraw into the castle and hardly ever show his face to the people again.

On March 20th, 1413, less than two decades after he had deposed Richard II, King Henry IV suffered a final attack at Westminster Abbey. He died in the Jerusalem Chamber after collapsing during his prayers at the shrine of St. Edward. He was buried opposite the grave of the Black Prince.

Henry IV was succeeded by his son, King Henry V, who has since been immortalized in Shakespeare's plays. And he was neither sick, nor mad, nor a mere boy, and that meant that he was ready for war.

Henry V had been well-prepared for war. He had fought at his father's side in the various rebellions, and as his father grew sicker and sicker, the younger Henry assumed more and more responsibility for the government. By the time the old king had died, Henry V was more than ready to take the throne.

A massively tall man for his era at 6' 3", Henry was strong and healthy, and he gave off an irresistible air of vitality. He was hungry to prove himself as a powerful warrior king just like Edward had been. While the peace had lasted for two decades, the opposing nations were by no means reconciled; France had lent much assistance and support to Henry IV's archenemy, Welsh rebel Owain Glyndwr. Henry's fingers were itching for power, and he was the first king since Edward who had an ambition for the French throne.

France was deeply divided as various princes struggled for control over the regency, and Henry was ready to strike at these weaknesses. He started by making demands on France, asking for the entirety of Aquitaine to be returned to his possession as per the terms of the Treaty of Brétigny. He also demanded the payment of more than one million crowns, a debt still outstanding from the ransom of King John the Good, Charles the Mad's grandfather. When he demanded to have the hand of Catherine of Valois—the daughter of King Charles—in marriage, the French drew the line. His demands were refused, and Henry prepared for war.

* * * *

Henry's army landed on the north banks of the River Seine on August 14th, 1415. He had with him about eight thousand men—a daunting prospect for the garrison of the nearby port town of Harfleur. Now a small town, Harfleur was then one of the most important ports in all of Normandy, and so it was fairly well defended with strong walls and outworks. However, its garrison numbered less than 250 men.

It must have been a terrifying sight for the hapless people of Harfleur as the horizon grew black with the approach of Henry's army. It was small consolation that reinforcements were coming: three hundred men arrived under the command of Raoul of Gaucourt, doubling the garrison, yet still a pitiful number compared to the might of the English army. Before more reinforcements could be called in, Henry's brother, Thomas, led part of the army across to the east of Harfleur, surrounding the town on the landward side and effectively sealing it off against all aid.

Now the siege could begin. Siege warfare was popular during the Middle Ages, a time when fortifications were a major part of defenses; many towns could not be penetrated, but they could be surrounded, and their inhabitants could be starved into submission.

During siege warfare, the attacking army would typically surround its unlucky target, digging trenches and building defenses of their own in order to create a safe space for the soldiers to live for several weeks, sometimes even months. The attackers would keep pressure on the besieged city by attempting to destroy its walls. This seldom succeeded in actually breaching the walls, but it did wear down the city's resources as men were killed in the attacks and much manpower and material were expended in an attempt to repair damage to the defenses. Attackers would use massive weapons known as siege engines in an attempt to bring down the walls. An example of these engines would include the mighty trebuchet, a massively tall object that towered over its operators and used a system of counterweights to launch large projectiles—usually rocks—over or directly into the city walls. Battering rams were also popular. These large, heavy objects, typically made of a single gigantic log, were used by groups of men to smash into doors in an attempt to break them down.

The defenders' castles were typically fortified not only with walls but also with battlements (defensible walkways on top of the walls from which soldiers could launch missiles of their own or even pour boiling oil on the attackers), arrowslits (tiny holes in the walls from which archers could fire on the enemy), and moats. These defenses were often good enough to withstand an attack for months, leading to drawn-out sieges that often ended simply because the city had run out of food and had no choice but to surrender.

Henry, however, was not interested in the archaic trebuchet. Instead, he was bringing with him a new weapon that had just begun to prove its use in warfare: the cannon.

The inhabitants of Harfleur knew that their defenses were strong and felt bolstered by the backup they had received from Raoul of Gaucourt. They were ready to face the two thousand archers and six thousand men-at-arms that Henry had brought with him, watching as the trenches were dug and wooden screens constructed to protect the operators of his heavy artillery. And then the first cannon spoke. A heavy crack filled the air, followed by the smell of gunpowder and the thin whine of a cannonball. It struck the walls with a devastating crunch, blowing a hole in the stone and causing the walls to shudder. But the French were not intimidated. They had guns of their own, and they dragged the heavy cannon up to the battlements and answered with a few shots of their own.

Outnumbered as they were—more than thirteen to one—the French were determined not to give up. Repairing their damaged city every night, they continued to fire on the English by day. Even when Henry grew desperate as the weeks wore on and sent miners to tunnel beneath the walls in the hopes of destroying the city from underneath, the French sent their own miners to dig tunnels right into those of the English and kill them. Meanwhile, the soldiers surrounding the town were starting to feel the effects of more than just the battle; with eight thousand people effectively camping in squalor so near to one another, it was inevitable that disease would spread rapidly through them. Dysentery likely killed more of the English during the siege than Frenchmen did.

And the Frenchmen fought courageously. August wore on into September, and the weather was starting to turn cold when finally the English succeeded in capturing the bulwarks outside the town's main gate. Dispirited, the French realized that they would have to negotiate or, potentially, the entire town could be put to death. The townsfolk of cities that surrendered were often spared; those who did not surrender were usually butchered. Knowing this, on September 18th, the commanders of the town agreed to surrender within the next four days unless they were relieved by a French army. The commanders had sent a message to the current Dauphin, Louis, asking for support. But it never came; Louis simply did not have enough men with him to defeat the might of the English. On September 22nd, Harfleur surrendered, its commanders ceremoniously handing the keys to the city over to King Henry.

The inhabitants of the town that agreed to swear fealty to King Henry were allowed to stay. But as for the rest, regardless of their age, they were sent off into the countryside with nowhere to go.

They found refuge in Rouen while Henry installed a large garrison at Harfleur, confident that this campaign would wipe away the memory of the ignominy of his grandfather John of Gaunt's failed chevauchée.

For the first time in decades, England had won a battle. The Hundred Years' War was back in full swing.

Chapter 13 – The Battle of Agincourt

Illustration V: The Battle of Agincourt

As the triumphant army marched from Harfleur, they could feel the first nip of winter in the air. The chill morning breezes testified to the fact that the summer months, so ideal for campaigning kings, were over; the snow was coming, and with it, increased risk of death and disease among the soldiers. The campaign season was coming to a close. Henry had hoped to be able to attack Paris directly after defeating Harfleur, thinking that if he could destroy the French capital, then the entire kingdom was all but his. However, the resilience of the residents of Harfleur had surprised him. They had held out for far longer than he had thought, and disease left his army reduced, the siege having drastically impacted his supplies.

Instead, Henry swung his army to the north, heading for the English stronghold of Calais. He likely planned to winter there before renewing his attack in the spring. His army still had to march there, however—a distance of hundreds of miles—and they were running low on food and money. Henry ordered them to raid and forage as they went, as to further decrease French resources.

The army headed north, aiming for Calais. Unbeknownst to them, the Dauphin Louis had finally finished putting together the army that was supposed to have relieved Harfleur. He watched the English movements closely, still reluctant to engage them in a pitched battle. Instead, he sent his army—a force of about nine thousand, similar to the size of Henry's—to follow the River Somme to prevent the English from crossing it.

By late October, the Somme was the largest obstacle standing between the English and their safe haven of Calais. Henry's men were sick and tired; they had marched more than two hundred miles in less than two weeks, and many of them were still suffering from the dysentery that had plagued them at Harfleur. They needed to get over the Somme and into Calais as quickly as possible because the French army was growing even as it followed them along the river. Louis had issued a call to the local nobles, encouraging them to join in the fight against the English; with every day the army grew, his confidence grew too. Now it was Henry that was trying to avoid a battle with his weary troops, but it soon became evident that there was going to be no escape. They needed to get to

Calais, and if they had to go through the French army to do it, then so be it.

On October 25th, 1415, the two armies came together at last in a narrow valley near the modern-day village of Azincourt, France. The English were only about twenty miles from their destination, but as many as 36,000 French soldiers lay between them and Calais. The French army, commanded by a handful of French dukes, consisted mostly of noblemen, and as they waited for the battle to begin, a little arrogance began to creep into their words and actions. They were starting to feel confident about the battle, knowing that they outnumbered the English three to one. What was more, Henry's army only numbered about 1,500 men-at-arms at best; the rest of the army was made up solely of longbowmen. The men-at-arms were generally of noble blood, while the archers were mere commoners, and the nobility thus barely considered them human—let alone warriors. The French crossbowmen and other common soldiers were kept back because the men-at-arms decided that they simply didn't need a bunch of peasants to help them win the battle.

They were sorely mistaken. As the long night stretched on, the French nobles told their common soldiers to stay back, telling them that there was no room for them in the battle. The English, by contrast, remained in utter silence—Henry had ordered them not to breathe a word all night in order to avoid a surprise attack and also to keep the men focused on what was to come. They would need every drop of their courage and brainpower to face the mighty French force.

Dawn broke, and nothing happened. Henry was reluctant to charge the French, knowing that holding a defensive position was generally a safer move. The French, by contrast, were well-fed and had ample food, as well as almost 9,000 reinforcements marching to meet them—they simply sat back and waited, knowing that they were preventing Henry from getting to safety. For three long and agonizing hours, Henry waited. At last, he knew that he would have to move before the French army grew even more or he lost more men to dysentery. He advanced his army, setting them in array between two forests on the flanks of the hills. Using the same battle plan that had been so successful at Crécy, Henry arrayed his men-at-arms at the center of a funnel formed by longbowmen. This time, the longbowmen were protected by sharpened wooden stakes that had been driven into the ground at an angle in front of them.

The move awakened the French's lust for battle. They mounted their horses and launched a cavalry charge directly toward the longbowmen, charging uphill toward the wooden stakes. Faced with a wall of horses coming at them, the longbowmen had to stand their ground and fire their arrows at the intimidating enemy. The arrows inflicted little damage to the knights, but they did wound many horses, cutting or puncturing their backs and flanks. This generally failed to kill them, but it did make them panic. Faced by a wall of stakes and driven wild with pain, the horses turned and fled back down the hillside in an out-of-control stampede that took them directly through the ranks of the French infantry. The infantry found themselves being trampled and killed by the horses of their own army. What was more, the charging horses' iron-shod feet served to plow up the muddy ground between the warring armies—a considerable disadvantage for the French.

Pulling back with their first charge repulsed, the French reconsidered. They realized that the unarmored horses would be useless against the longbowmen. Instead, they decided to advance on foot, with heavy plate armor protecting the men against the rain of English arrows. The army was divided into three columns or "battles," and the first one headed toward the English men-at-arms on foot. The mud slowed their first frantic rush to a kind of flounder through the mud; the slow-moving targets would have been easy pickings for the longbowmen, but as arrows continued to pour onto them, their advance went on. The sound of metal arrowheads striking plate armor must have been deafening, a roaring cacophony that shook the surrounding woods and hills. But the French went on, their armor holding, and reached the line of men-at-arms.

At this point, many of the longbowmen exchanged their bows for swords and axes and rushed forward. The French found themselves in a closing vise of enemies, all of them desperate to get to the safety of Calais, fighting tooth and nail in desperation. Soon the French line was scattered and struggling, broken up into knots of individuals who fought as hard as they could. But the army was not coherent, the command was fragmented, and without unity, it was nothing.

The second French battle rushed in to the aid of their comrades, and then did some of the third, but nothing worked. The longbowmen were fighting hand-to-hand now, others shooting at a range that could puncture plate armor, and the French were dying in the thousands.

The three French battles were all but destroyed. Those Frenchmen who were worth something were imprisoned for ransom; the others were killed. When the battle stilled at last, Henry had several thousand prisoners. Lifting his eyes from the battlefield, a sticky mess of mud and blood, he spotted the fresh French rearguard waiting in the distance. Fear filled him. He had too many prisoners, and if they realized this, then they could easily rise up and overwhelm the weary English. Worse, if that rearguard attacked, his men would be needed to withstand their charge rather than guard his prisoners.

Henry's decision was merciless. He ordered his knights to butcher the prisoners. They resisted—the idea went against every concept of the code of chivalry in which they had been raised. Enraged, the young king threatened to hang every one of his own warriors that failed to comply, and the knights turned on their prisoners and cut them down in the hundreds.

Now all that was left was to repel the remnants of the third French battle and the rearguard. Exhausted, Henry turned to his handful of mounted knights and ordered a charge. With most of their command dead and having just witnessed the massacre of their fellow men, the French were terrified. They fled, and the English ransacked their entire camp.

* * * *

The English were not without casualties during the Battle of Agincourt, with some high-ranking commanders—such as the Duke of York and the Earl of Suffolk—being killed. However, England only lost about six hundred men; France, on the other hand, lost as many as eleven thousand. Their giant army had been destroyed by a bunch of commoners, a crew of longbowmen whose only ambition was to get to Calais. The impact on the French nobility was enormous, with hundreds of high-ranking lords killed or captured during the battle.

With his enemy being almost annihilated, Henry was free to lead his tired, battered, and somewhat demoralized but victorious army to the safety of Calais. He himself would return to England in November and be received with open arms by a nation who had finally found a warrior king that they could see as a hero once more. France was not yet utterly defeated, but the English had someone to believe in, and their enemy was torn apart with its king gone mad and many of its noblemen killed in the battle.

But the war was far from over. Three-quarters of a century had passed since the young King Edward III had first paid homage to the King of France wearing a sword and a crown, and several decades were still to come before the fight would be over at last.

Chapter 14 – A Baby King

In 1417, Henry returned to France, this time with his gaze set on nothing but total victory. His army swept through Normandy, a land that had belonged to the English centuries ago, and one by one they captured its fortresses, including the important cities of Caen and Rouen. The alliance between France and Burgundy had been destroyed; in 1419, the Burgundians allied themselves to the new bully on the block and assisted England in seizing the entirety of Normandy.

By this point, France had lost most of its trust in its own nobility. King Charles was mad, Louis was dead, and supporters of the new Dauphin, also a Charles, had the Duke of Burgundy assassinated—a move that eventually led to Burgundy's alliance with England. The entire country hated him, and apart from that, the French were tired of decades upon decades of war. In 1420, with Henry apparently unstoppable as he charged through a country divided by mental illness and murder, King Charles agreed to meet with Henry in an attempt to come to a treaty.

It was less of a treaty than it was a humiliating capitulation, although France did not quite surrender completely. Somehow,

King Charles managed to get through the meeting without having a psychotic episode, which must have been a great relief to his courtiers, including his wife Isabeau of Bavaria. Still, he appeared to have had little to do with the negotiations, more or less agreeing to Henry's terms. Princess Catherine was handed over and given to Henry in marriage; but more than that, the Dauphin Charles was disinherited, and King Henry was named the successor to the French throne. Isabeau herself agreed to disinherit the Dauphin, feeling that Henry had proven himself a stronger ruler than either her son or her husband. The English had laid claim to France at last. These negotiations were made final and ratified in the Treaty of Troyes, which was signed on May 21st, 1420.

The war appeared to be over. But Henry's brother and heir apparent, Thomas the Duke of Clarence, was about to make a move that would jeopardize everything that Henry had worked so hard for.

* * * *

Even though Henry was now heir to the throne of France, the war wasn't over yet. Many regions of France had not yet submitted to the idea of someday being ruled by an Englishman, even though Henry was practically ruling the country already, as he had been declared regent. The main resistance was organized by the disinherited—and disgruntled—Dauphin.

Having established himself in Paris, however, Henry knew that things were as stable as he could hope for in France for the time being. He returned to England in 1421, leaving Thomas in charge of his latest conquest. In a bid to suppress the Dauphin's resistance against him, Henry ordered Thomas to go on a chevauchée in some of the French provinces. Giving him command of four thousand men for this purpose, Henry gave Thomas his orders and then headed back to England, leaving his brother to it.

Thomas and his men swept across the provinces of Anjou and Maine, effortlessly burning and pillaging anything that the Dauphin could still claim as his own. At first, no attempt was made to stop them; after fighting in the six-month siege of Rouen in 1418-1419, it must have felt like easy pickings to the battle-hardened Thomas. Compared to how hard the invasion of Normandy had been, this was a walk in the park.

The Dauphin, however, had not given up entirely. He turned to a fellow enemy of England, a country that had been France's ally for more than a century: Scotland. Having been at war with England for almost as long as France had been, the Scots were more than happy to help and had sent reinforcements to France as early as 1419. The Dauphin's army of 5,000 consisted mostly of Scots, and they were ready to taste some English blood.

Good Friday—March 21st, 1421—saw Thomas' army comfortably encamped near the village of Vieil Baugé. Thomas suspected that the Dauphin had an army somewhere nearby, but he wasn't too worried, deciding to send almost all of his archers out in small foraging parties to find potential targets and supplies. He kept with him approximately 1,500 of his nobility, the mounted men-at-arms, while allowing the commoners to do the scavenging.

But supplies weren't all that the foraging parties found. One of them came back wide-eyed and dragging prisoners with them, prisoners whose fire and accents marked them as Scottish. The scouts brought news of the large Franco-Scottish army encamped nearby. Thomas was delighted to finally have found something to fight after weeks of idle pillaging. Turning to his handful of knights, he rallied them together, deciding that this little force was going to attack and conquer the Dauphin's army by themselves. His advisers tried to persuade him to wait for the return of his archers, who made up nearly two-thirds of his army, but Thomas would not be swayed. He languidly bade the Earl of Salisbury to hang out at camp and wait for the archers to get back, then to follow him as soon as possible. Meanwhile, he was going to use the element of surprise and take on the Dauphin straight away. He was convinced his knights could do it.

He was also wrong. His knights, outnumbered four to one, followed him courageously, directly into the Franco-Scottish army. Their initial charge was almost successful, as the shocked Scots drew back for a moment. Upon seeing how small their opponent's force was, they quickly regrouped, and this time they were using a form of England's own deadliest weapon against it: archers. Scottish longbowmen had the same prowess as the English, and they shot down Thomas' foolish cavalry charge. What little remained of the cavalry crashed into a melee of hand-to-hand fighting in which it was utterly outnumbered and was quickly and bloodily overwhelmed.

It was a Scottish rider, Sir John Carmichael of Douglasdale, who unhorsed Thomas; he charged straight into the English heir with a force that shattered his own lance. Thomas crashed to the ground, where he was quickly set upon by Sir Alexander Buchanan, another Scot. Sir Alexander made quick work of him. Thomas was cut down and killed, and the army was practically destroyed. The Earl of Salisbury rescued what handfuls of men were left when the archers finally joined him, but it was too late. More than a thousand of the English knights were killed.

The Scots allowed the Earl to lead the rest of the army away and into the safety of Normandy, sorely beaten by the same arrogance that had cost the French so dearly at Agincourt. If they had pursued the English army, they might have cast them out of France once and for all. Either way, the Scots had proven themselves on the battlefield as a powerful ally of France, so much so that Pope Martin V semi-humorously commented on the Scottish being an excellent "antidote for the English."

* * * *

Henry took the news of his brother's death surprisingly well, but this didn't mean that he was going to neglect his duty to avenge his brother. His rivalry with the Dauphin had now become personal, and Henry was determined to firmly establish his kingship of France the moment that crazy old King Charles died. Having just finished dealing with the coronation of his new wife, now Queen Catherine, Henry sailed to Calais in June 1421 with an army of about 5,000 men.

Henry's goal was to destroy as many southern—mostly Dauphin-held—French towns as possible. This campaign started out successfully, but once again, the French proved their tenacity in siege warfare, and it took Henry seven months to conquer the fortified city of Meaux. Its walls came down at last in the spring of 1422.

With Meaux conquered, Henry planned to continue his campaign, but the reign of England's ruthless and ambitious king was about to be cut cruelly short. In August 1422, while on campaign, he became suddenly and dramatically sick. He had dysentery, that same illness that had claimed so many of his men at the Siege of Harfleur. This form of infectious diarrhea had also taken the life of the Black Prince, and Henry would share the same fate. He died on August 31st, leaving behind only a single heir: an eight-month-old baby boy, Henry's first child to Catherine, the princess of France.

Little Henry VI was only nine months old when he was crowned the king of England. And less than two months after that, King Charles the Mad died peacefully of an illness, potentially malaria. He had been the mad king for nearly thirty years of his forty-two-year reign, and his death meant that the ten-month-old Henry VI was now the king of both England and France.

Because the baby king was unable to rule, responsibility for France fell to his uncle, John of Lancaster, the Duke of Bedford. His main goal was to get rid of the Dauphin, who still believed that he was the rightful king instead of this little babe who had no idea of the power that he already held. The Dauphin Charles was determined to reclaim his throne, but the Duke of Bedford was an able commander who led his army to several victories against the Dauphin. The most notable of these was the Battle of Verneuil on August 17th, 1424, in which the Dauphin's entire army was more or less destroyed. The Duke of Bedford was sensible enough to use his archers well, and this resulted in the loss of about half the Dauphin's army.

This left the Dauphin to retreat to the town of Bourges, south of the Loire River. He called himself the King of France, while his enemies mocked him by calling him the King of Bourges instead because that was about all the land that Charles controlled at that point. In fact, he was thinking of fleeing to Castile, giving up on the kingdom that he had one day been poised to inherit. As the fourth son of King Charles VI, the Dauphin had had to outlive all his older brothers in order to come to power; to have it so cruelly taken from him now was more than he could bear.

Yet all was not lost for the lost king. Help was about to come from the most unlikely source.

Chapter 15 – Joan and the Siege

Illustration VI: Joan of Arc

She was just a peasant girl. She wasn't supposed to be important.

She wasn't supposed to change the course of the war.

* * * *

Joan was born into a time when women were regarded more as objects than as people. As evidenced by Princess Catherine's betrothal to King Henry V, high-born women were used as trading pieces in the politics of this era; they were pieces of property, sometimes to be admired, sometimes to be boasted of, but never, ever to act of their own accord. Certainly, they were never allowed to go to war. And as for peasant women, they were little more than beasts of burden, not even useful for battles as their male counterparts were. They were nothing.

Yet a young peasant girl born in 1412 in a nondescript little French village was about to change the outcome of the war—and to impact history forever.

Joan was the daughter of a pair of farmers, typical peasant people who raised her to be a typical young peasant girl. She couldn't read or write, nor had she ever been taught to wield a weapon. Instead, her mother taught her to milk cows, tend flocks, and to worship God. And according to Joan, it was this same God who would change her life and the course of history.

Joan was thirteen when she first met the saints. They appeared to her as she was working in her mother's garden, three of them whose faces she recognized from pictures at church, and they told her that she was going to save France and reinstate its rightful king. The saints disappeared, and Joan took their words with great seriousness. She vowed to devote herself to the service of God until He saw fit to send her forth into battle.

The time came in May 1428, at a time when France was in dire need of rescue. The Duke of Bedford had brought the entirety of northern France, as well as its southwestern coast, to its knees; only the center of the country remained under the control of those loyal to the House of Valois and thus to the Dauphin Charles. The English army was ready to head into central France and take the entire country for Henry VI, who was then a six-year-old child. Only one major obstacle was left: Orléans. This major city was located on the banks of the Loire, and it was the northernmost city that remained under Charles' control. If Orléans could be taken, the rest of France was as good as defeated.

The Earl of Salisbury, who was in command of the English army, led a force of English and Burgundian troops against Orléans in the autumn of 1428. At first, it seemed the siege would be brief. The Tourelles, or gatehouse, of the city fell within the first few weeks; the entire city would have been lost if not for the timely arrival of some French reinforcements. The French dug in, and so did the English. The siege became a waiting game. For four long months, the citizens of Orléans lived in the shadow of the enemy, slowly starving as they waited for the warring armies to come to some kind of a crisis.

The crisis came in February 1429 when a Franco-Scottish army arrived to relieve the besieged city. They attacked a convoy of English supply wagons destined for the troops surrounding Orléans, but the fight was a devastating defeat known as the Battle of Herrings, in which the English sent the French and their allies fleeing and triumphantly continued on to Orléans, supplies and all. Dismayed that not even the supply convoy could be stopped, let alone the besieging army, the commanders of the city decided that it was time to surrender.

They offered to turn the entire city over to Philip III the Good, Duke of Burgundy, as well as giving a portion of their taxes to the English and allowing the army to pass through Orléans and continue on to Bourges. The Duke of Burgundy found the offer irresistible, but he knew that he would have to get the proposal past the Duke of Bedford first. As much as Bedford was tempted by the offer, he knew that striking Bourges directly would mean final victory, so he declined. He felt that Orléans was going to fall sooner rather than later, and he had no need to make compromises. It was going to be everything or nothing.

The Duke of Bedford's decision turned out to be a mistake. Joan of Arc was coming, and she was going to change everything.

* * * *

As the Battle of Herrings raged, Joan of Arc was fighting a battle of her own—but this was a battle of wits, not weapons.

She was sixteen years old now, and she believed she had heard the voice of God. He told her that it was time to go and find the Dauphin Charles and crown him king in Reims, then to liberate the French people from the cruel grip of the English. Joan did not protest, nor did she look to her lowborn status as an excuse. Instead, she went to the nearest Dauphinois captain that she could find and simply explained the matter to him.

Captain Robert de Baudricourt almost laughed aloud at this sweet-looking little peasant girl who dared to demand an audience with the king. He sent her off with some sarcastic remark, shaking his head and believing that he'd never see her again. But Joan did not give up. She came to him again and again, finally telling him that God had shown her how the Dauphin's troops had suffered a defeat that very day. Baudricourt dismissed her—until he learned of the Battle of Herrings. The fact that Joan had apparently known about the defeat long before any means could have brought the news to her convinced him that this girl really was some kind of warrior prophet. He agreed to take her to Chinon where the Dauphin was staying at the time.

Dressed as a man to survive the eleven-day journey across territory crawling with vengeful English, Joan and her escort arrived in Chinon in early March. It was a few days before she was granted a private audience with the Dauphin. Although initially skeptical, he agreed to hear her out—and what she said convinced him that she was heaven-sent. Nobody knows what exactly she told him; it was all uttered in the strictest confidence, but whatever it was, it changed his mind. Once Charles had her cross-examined by the church at

Poitiers to ensure that Joan's visions came from God and not from darker places, he accepted her as a prophet. The church, however, was convinced that she was a Christian, but not that she was the prophet she claimed to be. They told Charles that he would have to test her, to see if she really had a divine blessing.

Charles could see one easy and simple way to carry out this test. The girl kept telling him that she was going to relieve Orléans, that God was going to help her to do it. The city was all but lost already; what was one more peasant girl in the face of so many casualties?

He let her go. And dressed in a new suit of plate armor, astride a plunging warhorse, Joan of Arc went.

* * * *

The residents of Orléans knew all of the stories that had been circulating France for the past few years. There were prophecies about someone who was going to come, someone that God was going to send to save them from the English. The prophecies were vague, but they all seemed to involve the same thing: a girl dressed in armor.

And on April 29th, the prophecy came true in the eyes of everyone stuck in besieged Orléans. First, they saw a banner: a shining, white banner, snapping in the evening wind. Then they saw the girl. She was young, her skin smooth and fair, but her eyes ablaze with something that seemed to be beyond the very concept of time. Her armor gleamed the purest white in the dusk, and so did the flanks of the proud horse that bore her. And the fire in her eyes—something about it lit up everything inside all who beheld her.

It was Joan. She had managed to get into the city at last, after days of deception from commanders who did not take this teenage peasant seriously and kept coming up with false reasons for why she could not go in. And now that she was finally there, she was about to get busy.

In short, over the next week, Joan led the French army to victory. How exactly she achieved this is a subject that has puzzled historians for centuries. Joan did not bear a sword, nor did she shed enemy blood; instead, she carried only her shining white banner, and she rode unarmed into the fray on her beautiful white horse. And the French army fixed their eyes on her, and they followed her into the trenches. On May 4th, they attacked and defeated an outlying fortress; the day after, yet another. By May 7th, they had taken the Tourelles back. Joan was wounded by an English arrow, yet she continued to ride on ahead, and by this point, the French would have followed her through the very fires of Hell if she chose to lead them there. Instead, she led them to the English. With the Tourelles gone, Orléans could be resupplied easily, and so the siege was over. The English retreated.

Joan left Orléans not long after; once her wound had a little time to recover, she turned her white horse back toward Tours, where she planned to meet with the Dauphin. She was going to proclaim her victory, but she also had other plans. That sad-eyed prince had been a prince for too long. Joan was going to make him king if it was the last thing she did.

And sadly, it almost would be.

Chapter 16 – The Last Battles

After Orléans found itself suddenly and stunningly liberated, all of France rallied behind the banner of Joan, now nicknamed the Maid of Orléans. The English, startled by this sudden comeback, were pushed back with surprising ease as Joan and the commander of the majority of Charles' army, the Duke of Alençon, proceeded to take the bridges along the Loire River to prevent the English from carrying out their plan of capturing central France. With their border defended, the French went on the offensive, and the English braced themselves for an invasion.

The English expected that the French would turn toward Normandy or Paris next. Instead, to their surprise, Joan, Alençon, and the Dauphin set their sights on Reims. It was a risky idea, much farther into enemy territory than the more strategically important capital at Paris, but Joan was determined: Charles needed to be crowned king, and it would be done at Reims, where it had always been done. While Charles was still somewhat reluctant to trust her, Alençon supported her fully, and he followed every piece of her advice in his command. The two of them headed toward Reims, their army's morale rising with every victory. Three cities fell before them within five days that summer, and it was enough to convince Charles to follow them to the city. He was finally crowned King Charles VII on July 17th, 1429.

After King Charles' coronation, things took a turn for the worse. Giddy on the sweet savor of victory, the king followed Joan to Paris, where they laid siege to the city in an attempt to take the capital back. The siege was brief, ambitious, and a complete failure. Joan led a courageous group of men to the very gates of Paris, where the Parisians met them with a rain of crossbow bolts; one such bolt pierced Joan's thigh, and the wounded warrior maiden was carried from the field. With the white banner fallen, the men fell back, and when it became evident that Paris was not going to surrender, Charles decided to withdraw his army.

Joan was incensed. She had wanted to renew the assault, but Charles stood firm, taking his men back to the lands south of the Loire where everything was still under his control. Joan, however, went northward to the town of Compiègne instead. Despite being deep in English territory, the town had just declared its loyalty to King Charles, and Joan knew it was only a matter of time before the English would try to crush its resistance.

Charles had lost faith in Joan after the failed siege of Paris, so he refused to give her any support. Instead, she took it upon herself to rally support of her own. The French still believed in the Maid of Orléans, and she headed to Compiègne with a band of about four hundred volunteers.

Before the city could be fully besieged, Joan attempted a short offensive, launching a surprise attack on a nearby Burgundian outpost with the assistance of a Frenchman, Guillaume de Flavy. Before the attack could fully commence, however, a passing enemy count happened to notice Joan's army, and reinforcements were called in. They arrived with a speed and strength that Joan knew her little band of volunteers could not defeat. She ordered them to pull back to Compiègne and save themselves. They rushed back toward the town; Joan, however, reined in her horse, waiting for every man to be on his way back to safety before she followed. It was the position of honor taken by all great commanders in retreat, and it was her custom to do so, even though she bore no weapons and could make no attempt to protect the rear of her small army.

Still, she would have made it to safety, if it was not for Guillaume de Flavy. Seeing the pursuing Burgundians hot on the heels of the French, Guillaume decided to cut his losses—even if it meant losing some of his rearguard. He led the troops into Compiègne and then, right before Joan's horrified eyes, he slammed the gates shut. The rearguard piled up against the gates, pounding on them, screaming at their commander to open up, to let them into safety even as the Burgundians bore down upon them. But Guillaume did no such thing. He watched as the Burgundians overwhelmed and captured the rearguard, including their illustrious leader, Joan of Arc.

* * * *

The Burgundians were overjoyed to have captured such an important figure in the French army. They carried Joan off to a nearby fortress and held her prisoner, despite her many attempts to escape. She was a troublesome prisoner, and when the English offered 10,000 livres tournois to buy her from the Burgundians, they gladly sold her as if she was an inanimate object.

The English promptly put Joan on trial. In a sad twist of fate, the girl who claimed to be sent by God was tried as a witch, and because the trial was overseen entirely by Englishmen and Burgundians who knew what she meant to their French enemies, they were determined to prove her guilty. Joan was burned at the stake in the city of Rouen on May 30th, 1431. She had only one final request: for a crucifix to be held before her as she burned to death.

Almost five hundred years later, in 1909, Joan was not only rehabilitated into the church —she was beatified. In the Catholic Church, she is now known as Saint Joan.

* * * *

Joan was gone, but France's war was far from over. The tide had already turned against the English, and despite the defeats at Paris and Compiègne, the French were slowly winning back the territories that England had claimed. When the Duke of Bedford died in 1435—ninety-eight years after the war began—it was a heavy blow to the English; King Henry VI was still only a little boy, and England found itself without a leader to speak of. Charles VII, meanwhile, was determined to finally get himself onto the throne in Paris. In an act that once again portrayed the fickleness of Burgundy, the Duke of Burgundy made Charles' wish come true in September 1435 by deserting England in favor of France and signing a treaty that would return Paris to Charles' control.

King Charles was on his throne at last. And England, floundering without leadership, was gradually forced out of the country over the next eighteen years. Rouen fell in 1449; the rest of Normandy not long after. With Normandy back under his control, King Charles decided to set his sights on Gascony, the duchy that had started this whole long mess of a war. Bordeaux, the capital, fell to France in 1451. Its citizens had been considering themselves subjects of the English king for centuries and were not amused by this sudden turn of events. They turned to Henry VI, by now an adult, for assistance. He was too busy concentrating on expanding his territories elsewhere and could hardly be bothered by this old war in France, so he sent an army of about 3,000 men under the aging John Talbot, Earl of Shrewsbury. He still managed to retake the city in October 1452.

Unlike Henry VI, Charles was utterly focused on winning the war and driving the pesky English out of France forever. As Talbot advanced from Bordeaux, Charles' army drew nearer to him, ready to block whatever move he might make. On July 17th, 1453, Charles set his army in array against Talbot's. His battle was eerily similar to the stance taken by the English at the Battle of Crécy, with one major difference: Charles was not using longbowmen—he was using guns. With as many as three hundred guns waiting for the arrival of Talbot's little army, Charles knew that the victory was his before the battle had even begun.

Talbot advanced, a sixty-six-year-old man with a white beard and a mind full of knights, archers, and other dated methods of warfare. But the time of the English longbowmen was over. French artillery was the best in the world now; bows and arrows were outdated, and the smell of gunpowder and the crack of guns had replaced the clatter of arrows raining down on steel. Talbot's men advanced straight into a rain of utter death, with a single cannon shot being reported to have killed as many as six men at a time. Carnage ruled among the troops, Talbot was killed, and the English were utterly routed.

The Battle of Castillon marked the official end of the Hundred Years' War, with a decisive French victory assuring that the duchy of Gascony was returned to the French crown, Calais being the only English territory left. The age of armored knights wielding lances and broadswords, accompanied by feudal recruits who shot wooden arrows from bows that had been carved from a single piece of wood, was over. Now the armies would resemble that of the victorious Charles VII: professional military groups that carried guns and fought with cannons. The Hundred Years' War was over, and with it, the Middle Ages themselves were coming to a close.

Conclusion

One of the most important effects of the Hundred Years' War was to form a cultural divide between England and France for the first time. Ever since William the Conqueror landed on English soil, defeated King Harold at Hastings, and made England his own in 1066, England had been using the French language for all official business. It was only when the war had been raging for decades that the English language really came into its own for the first time—a language that still dominates the entire world today.

The population of both countries was also profoundly affected, with France losing as much as half its population to the combination of the Hundred Years' War and the Black Death.

Ultimately, however, the war's greatest effect was likely on warfare itself. The age of the knight and warhorse was drawn to a close during this war, with artillery, infantry, and light cavalry coming to the fore. The war also saw the development of the use of guns, which is easily evident when comparing the importance of cannons in early battles to later battles. At Crécy, cannons were more or less used only to intimidate the enemy, while at Castillon, they were instrumental to Charles VII's victory.

Perhaps one of the most important lessons to take away from the story of the war is how the greed and ambition of a single individual can cause strife, misery, and death across generations and throughout multiple countries. This war was not based on profound cultural differences. It was based on one simple thing: the pride and greed of King Edward III, for whom ruling over one country was simply not enough. He wanted the crown of France, he wanted to avoid the humiliation of paying homage to the king of France, and because of his arrogance and selfishness, two nations were plunged into an entire century of war.

Appendix: Comprehensive Timeline of the Hundred Years' War

The Edwardian War (1337-1360)

- **1328**: King Charles IV of France dies without an heir. Philip of Valois is crowned King Philip VI of France.
- **1330**: King Edward III of England is crowned and lays claim to the throne of France through his mother, Charles IV's sister Isabella.
- **1331**: Edward briefly accepts Philip VI as his liege, considering that Edward is also Duke of Aquitaine, a part of France.
- **1332**: Edward goes to war with David II of Scotland, who is a French ally.
- **1336**: Philip sends troops to Scotland to support David in the war on England. French privateers start to capture English ships.

- **1337**: Parliament approves Edward's plans to send an army to Aquitaine (also known as Gascony) after Philip confiscates some of Edward's French lands. Philip sounds a call to arms throughout France. Edward's army sets sail for Aquitaine in the middle of the year.
- **1340**: Edward makes his claim to the French throne public. England wins the Battle of Sluys.
- **1341**: The War of the Breton Succession begins, with England backing John of Montfort and France backing Charles of Blois.
- **1346**: England wins the Battle of Crécy in France and the Battle of Neville's Cross against the Scottish.
- **1347**: Edward takes Calais, a French fortress.
- **1348**: France is stricken by bubonic plague, bringing a pause to the war.
- **1350**: The plague kills Philip VI. King John II of France is crowned.
- **1356**: The Black Prince defeats King John II at the Battle of Poitiers; the French king is taken prisoner.
- **1358**: As the Dauphin Charles attempts to raise money to ransom his father the King of France, French peasants revolt against the raised taxes.
- **1359**: Charles is forced to refuse to accept a treaty proposed by the imprisoned King John due to financial strain.
- **1360**: Edward launches a campaign across France. Black Monday forces Edward to negotiate rather than press home his advantage. The Treaty of Brétigny is signed, handing over Aquitaine to England but renouncing Edward's claim to the French throne.

- **1364:** While there is peace between England and France, the War of the Breton Succession ends with the Battle of Auray. John of Montfort becomes Duke of Brittany. King John dies in captivity. King Charles V of France is crowned.
- **1366:** The Black Prince plays a role in the Castilian Civil War, assisting Pedro the Cruel against the French favorite, Henry of Trastámara. Pedro is reinstated but fails to pay his debts to the Black Prince.

The Caroline War (1369-1389)

- **1369:** Aided by France, Henry retakes the throne. The Black Prince harshly taxes Aquitaine; its lords appeal to Charles V for help, and war is declared.
- **1369:** A skirmish at Poitou results in the death of English Seneschal Sir John Chandos.
- **1372:** The French recapture Poitiers, La Rochelle, and other territories.
- **1373:** English Prince John of Gaunt leads a raid across France, which is ultimately a failure.
- **1376:** The death of the Black Prince.
- **1377:** The French recapture Bergerac. King Edward III dies and is succeeded by the boy king Richard II.
- **1380:** The English Earl of Buckingham raids France again in support of the Duke of Brittany, laying siege to Nantes. Charles V dies, and the young King Charles VI is crowned.
- **1381:** The Duke of Brittany switches sides and pays the Earl of Buckingham off to stop the offensive. The Peasants' Revolt in England distracts Richard II's attention from the war.

- **1382:** More peasant revolts in France continue to stall the war.
- **1383-1385:** The Portuguese interregnum, considered a proxy war.
- **1389:** Signing of the Truce of Leulinghem, beginning the second peace.
- **1392:** Charles VI goes mad.
- **1399:** Henry of Bolingbroke deposes Richard II and is crowned King Henry IV of England.
- **1400:** Wales starts a rebellion against England.
- **1402:** English invasion of Scotland, which results in the Percy Rebellion.
- **1405:** France supports Wales' rebellion.
- **1410:** Civil war threatens in France.
- **1413:** Henry IV dies. Henry V is crowned king of England. Seeing France is crippled under its mad king, Henry V lays claim to more territories in France and demands the hand of its princess in marriage.
- **1415:** Welsh rebellion crushed by the English.

The Lancastrian War (1415-1453)

- **1415:** Henry invades France. England wins the Siege of Harfleur and the Battle of Agincourt.
- **1417:** Caen falls to the English.
- **1419:** Rouen falls to the English.
- **1420:** Signing of the Treaty of Troyes. Henry marries the princess of France. The Dauphin, Charles, is disinherited.
- **1422:** Death of Henry V. Henry VI, a baby, is crowned king of England and of France. The Dauphin Charles tries to maintain control over central France.

- **1428:** The Siege of Orlèans begins. Joan of Arc receives her vision and begins to make attempts to reach the city.
- **1429:** Joan of Arc leads the French to victory at Orlèans, then crowns the Dauphin as King Charles VII in Reims.
- **1430:** Capture of Joan of Arc.
- **1431:** Joan of Arc is executed by the English.
- **1435:** Burgundy, a key ally of the English, allies itself to France instead.
- **1449:** Rouen recaptured by the French.
- **1450:** English defeated at the Battle of Formigny.
- **1451:** Territories in Aquitaine are reclaimed by the French.
- **1453:** Battle of Castillon ends in English defeat.

Part 2: Joan of Arc

A Captivating Guide to a Heroine of France and Her Role During the Lancastrian Phase of the Hundred Years' War

Introduction

Joan of Arc. Some see her as a lunatic; some, as a sadly misunderstood piece of history; others, as a power-hungry genius; and the Catholic Church, as a saint and a symbol of faith, humility, and courage in the face of persecution. Yet one thing cannot be denied: Joan of Arc was one of the most remarkable figures in the story of the human race, and her extraordinary life is a fascinating tale that leaves many questions unanswered by history.

When Joan arrived on the scene, France was a country in dire straits. Almost completely defeated by the English, it was on the very brink of becoming little more than a jewel in the English crown. The rightful heir to its throne, the Dauphin Charles, was a dispirited and morose man who had given up on ever ruling his country. The time had never been more ripe for a savior, and yet no savior had ever been as unlikely as Joan. She was no warrior, nor was she a princess, nor was she educated in any way. Instead, she was just a peasant and a woman besides. In the medieval era, such a person was of practically no consequence.

Except Joan didn't let that stop her. Inspired by what she believed to be divine revelation, she dared to demand an audience with the Dauphin, even though she was of the lowest birth imaginable. She might not have been able to read or write, yet she was determined to save her country. It has been said that faith can move mountains. It is difficult to imagine a bigger mountain than the one that the faith of Joan moved.

Joan's story almost feels like a novel instead of a part of history. She was a shining savior on a warhorse, waving her white banner and calling her soldiers forth to victory; but she was also painfully and intensely human, a young girl who wept and bled just the same as the rest of us. In the same breath, it is as easy to relate to Joan as it is to be awed by her incredible character. She may have been beatified as a saint, but Joan of Arc was in many ways a very ordinary human being, a person who felt pain and fear, a person who made mistakes and who had moments of weakness. This book follows her through her extraordinary journey. Feel her terror as she first experienced her visions. See her determination as she convinced a cynical captain to grant her passage to the Dauphin. Experience her exhilaration and faith as she led the French army to victory after victory. Weep alongside her as the King of France betrayed her. Suffer with her during her long imprisonment in the hands of her enemies. And cry with the witnesses who saw her burn for a crime she did not commit.

She was Joan of Arc, a person whose life remains wreathed in mystery, but nonetheless a fascinating adventure. And this is her story.

Chapter 1 – The Unending War

It all started with a baby—a baby girl, to be exact. If the tiny, newborn Blanche of France, born on April 1ˢᵗ, 1328, had just come into the world as a bouncing baby boy instead of a little girl, then the war might never have started. It was a twisted thing that such a small kink of fate should have the capacity to cause such widespread and enduring tragedy—and if it was not for the sexist laws of the era, as there would have been no conflict over the throne of France. Yet Blanche, the youngest of King Charles IV's two surviving daughters, happened to be born in a time when a woman was not allowed to rule the kingdom of France. And so, it was declared that Blanche's late father had died without an heir. The Capetian dynasty ended with him.

King Charles IV was the youngest surviving son of Philip IV, who had three boys. Each had been king in his turn after Philip's death: first Louis X, then Philip V, and then, finally, Charles. The only other siblings that were left were an older sister, Margaret, and a younger one, Isabella. Charles's younger brother Robert had died as a boy. Again because of their gender, neither of the women could take the throne. But perhaps Isabella could provide an heir—an heir that would be most unsatisfying to the French nobility. In a bid to improve diplomatic relations between France and England, Isabella had been married off to the prince of England when she was only twelve years old. But now she was a grown woman in her thirties, a fiercely intelligent one who had earned the title of She-Wolf of France, and her husband was the teenaged King Edward II of England. As the closest male relative of the late king of France, Edward had a legitimate claim to the French throne.

The French nobility scrambled to prevent the unthinkable of one man being the king of both France and England. They managed to come up with an alternative heir. Philip of Valois had been a fairly minor noble as the son of a count; much of his life prior to the death of King Charles IV has been lost to history as he was not considered important during his childhood. But his father, while a minor noble, was also the youngest brother of Philip IV—Charles IV's father—which made Philip of Valois the closest relative to the deceased king through the male line. He was hurriedly crowned King Philip VI of France before Edward could lay claim to the throne.

To rub salt in the wound, Edward was not only King of England but also Duke of Aquitaine—a large duchy in France—due to the fact that the kings of England had long owed their heritage to French blood since William the Conqueror's victories in 1066. For that reason, Edward was also technically a vassal of the king of France, which forced him to pay homage to the king. Paying homage was a humiliating ceremony that involved swearing allegiance and showing submission, and Edward did not intend to pay homage to a king that he believed had stolen his second throne.

Isabella had been married off to Edward in an attempt to make peace. In a horrible twist of fate, that very act ended up sparking the longest conflict in European history. It didn't take long for Edward, a hotheaded teenager, to violate the homage ceremony by wearing his sword and crown instead of being bareheaded as was custom. In retaliation, Philip attempted to confiscate Aquitaine. Edward accepted the challenge by forcing his claim to the French throne. In 1337, the call to arms was sounded. It was war.

* * * *

The Hundred Years' War has since become known as one of the longest conflicts in the history of the world. Up until World War I claimed that title, it was also known as the Great War. Starting in 1337, it would remain primarily a conflict over succession, raging between the English Plantagenet family and the French House of Valois. The amount of vitriol and combat that the war entailed eventually overflowed into several proxy wars, including the War of the Breton Succession and the Castilian Civil War, during which France and England would each pick a side and lend support to whichever champion they had chosen.

The first major battle, the Battle of Sluys in 1340, was a naval battle which was decisively won by the English, allowing them to invade France and lay siege to the fortress of Tournai. France fought back, attacking England on three fronts: in France itself, along the English coastline by burning and plundering several cities, and from the Scottish border via one of the most important French allies—King David I of Scotland.

However, as the first phase of the war stretched into the decades, England started to seize the upper hand. The English won the Battle of Crécy using the prowess of common longbowmen to defeat the magnificent French cavalry, an ignominious defeat for the haughty French. This was followed by more English victories at Neville's Cross and Calais, and then, finally—after a brief interlude while both countries were occupied with facing the Black Plague—Poitiers. This last victory resulted in the capture of the French king, Philip VI's successor John II. John was shipped back to England and ransomed for a ridiculous sum of money.

In 1360, King Edward led another campaign through crippled France. The country was struggling under its young leader, the Dauphin Charles, whose efforts were focused on taxing the peasants in order to be able to pay his father's ransom. Edward swept across the country, heading for Reims and Paris, two of France's most important cities. But Black Monday put a stop to all of that. A freak hailstorm broke out above Edward's troops, killing several thousand men and horses. Edward took this as a sign from God that this campaign was against His will and returned to England, resulting in the first treaty of the war. The Treaty of Brétigny renounced Edward's claim to the throne but restored Aquitaine to his possession. King Edward returned to England, leaving his son, Edward the Black Prince, in charge of Aquitaine.

The peace did not last long. The second phase of the war (known as the Caroline War) began only nine years later. The Black Prince's involvement in the Castilian Civil War had left him physically ill and financially crippled, forcing him to heavily tax his subjects in Aquitaine. King Edward III was getting old and sick himself, and King John II had finally died in captivity. His son was crowned Charles V. When some of the Black Prince's nobles from Aquitaine appealed to King Charles for help, the French king was delighted. He extended a polite summons to the Black Prince requesting his presence at France, whereupon the Prince declared that he would be there—with an invading army. All-out war began again.

This time, the French had the upper hand. With England's two most important military leaders incapacitated by age and illness, France was led by an angry king who had been waiting for this opportunity for far too long. By 1372, several territories were back under French control, including Poitiers and the important port town of La Rochelle. Raids by Englishmen John of Gaunt and the Earl of Buckingham proved ineffective as the French continued to recapture their lost ground.

When the Black Prince, King Edward, and King Charles died in 1376, 1377, and 1380, respectively, they were succeeded by two boy kings: ten-year-old Richard II of England and eleven-year-old Charles VI of France. Their youth and significant civil unrest—such as the English Peasants' Revolt in 1381—brought a sudden end to the hostilities. While the 1383-1385 Portuguese interregnum was considered a proxy war, it did not have a significant strategic effect, and by 1389, the kings had signed the Truce of Leulinghem, ending the Caroline phase of the war and ushering in 25 years of uneasy peace.

Perhaps some believed that the war might even be over. Yet unrest continued in both countries. In 1392, Charles VI suddenly and unexpectedly experienced a moment of psychosis that caused him to kill one of his own knights. He was dragged back to his castle in bonds for his own safety, and sadly for his people, this would not be the last of these episodes. He would continue to experience hallucinations, delusions, and strange behavior for the rest of his life. Without a ruler, France found itself unable to do much fighting on a grand scale.

England itself was in no position to invade, either. Richard II was deposed by Henry of Bolingbroke, soon crowned Henry IV, who was surrounded on all sides by rebellions from England and Wales. France supported the Welsh rebellion, but it was crushed in 1415 by Henry IV's son, a particularly ruthless young man crowned King Henry V in 1413.

With peace established in his own country, Henry V set his sights on expanding his rule. And he knew that France, with its mad king, was a sitting duck.

Chapter 2 – A Whispered Prophecy

The house where Joan of Arc was born
Arnaud 25, CC BY-SA 4.0 <https://creativecommons.org/licenses/by-sa/4.0>, via Wikimedia Commons https://commons.wikimedia.org/wiki/File:Maison_natale_Jeanne_d%27Arc_023.jpg

France, 1415. Harfleur had just fallen to the English. The port had put up a courageous resistance, resulting in a siege that lasted over a month, despite Henry V's significantly superior forces. But on September 22nd, the city fell at last, and Henry established a firm foothold on French soil where he could receive reinforcements.

All of France trembled in its boots. There were several strong French military leaders at the time, but King Charles VI's bouts of madness had only intensified and become more frequent as age continued to take a toll on his poor mental health. Without a single unifying leader, the French army was floundering in the face of Henry's mighty force. Henry attacked with single-minded determination while the French nobility squabbled arrogantly among themselves, and the commoners found themselves over-taxed and uninspired by their leadership. Many French nobles were starting to wonder if it wouldn't be better to just surrender to the English and allow themselves to be led by a king who was in full possession of his mental faculties, as well as being a gifted military leader.

But the commoners and many of the other nobles would have none of it. They were French, and they wanted to stay Frenchmen under a French king. And it was among these people that the prophecy had first started to circulate.

* * * *

As the English moved inexorably across the country, the prophecy flew from mouth to mouth. It was an old one, one that had long been recited, but the closer the English came, the faster the prophecy moved. A swift and whispered thing, it fled before the approaching horde.

No one is quite sure where the prophecy originally came from. Some attributed it to Saint Bede the Venerable, a monk and writer from the seventh century. Others believed it came from Euglide of Hungary, and still others thought it had been made by the mystical wizard from the time of King Arthur and his knights—Merlin. Wherever it came from and however old it was (no one knew for sure), it was suddenly remembered now. It was a desperate thing for a desperate time. And times grew ever more desperate as Henry swept across the country. City after city fell before him like wheat before the scythe, starting with the Battle of Agincourt, where the enormous French force could do nothing against the English. Caen fell. Then Rouen. By 1420, all of France was in great peril with the English swarming all over the countryside.

As fast as the English moved, the prophecy moved faster. It was on every set of lips and in every Frenchman's ear at that time. It was as simple as it was terrifying, as ominous as it was hopeful.

France will be lost by a woman, it said. *But it will be saved by a virgin from the borders of Lorraine.*

It was a strange prophecy for that time, considering that women were largely considered to have little role in politics and certainly no role in war. Even noblewomen were often used as a commodity at that time, being married off to improve alliances at their father's whim. Yet this prophecy seemed to say that two women would be able to change the fate of the whole of France, not once, but twice.

Perhaps at any other time, the prophecy would have been rejected. But not at this one. The people of France were desperate, and they clung to this prophecy with an iron grip.

* * * *

The French were well aware that the first part of their prophecy was about to come true—the part about France being lost by a woman. John the Fearless, Duke of Burgundy, had the potential to be one of France's key allies; but when jealous supporters of the Dauphin, also named Charles, assassinated him in Paris in 1419, the Burgundians switched sides to join forces with the English. Burgundy took Paris, and the capital was officially in the grasp of the enemy.

What the French didn't know was that the second part of the prophecy had already been set in motion. In 1412, even before Henry had landed in Harfleur, the Maid of France was born. Yet she was not born into the silken bedding of a noble house. Instead, she was brought forth in the peasant village of Domrémy in a modest but fairly typical peasant home—a crooked little building on a crooked little piece of pavement, bordered by the woods and the church. It was here, and not in some soaring palace or majestic castle, that the hero of France would spend her childhood. Domrémy itself was a small village of little consequence in the northeast of France near the border of Lorraine, then part of the Holy Roman Empire.

Jacques d'Arc was a farmer and a pillar of the community in the little village. He had some official duties in the village which helped to supplement his income on his small farm. His wife, Isabelle, was a housewife, as was typical of peasant women in this period, but she showed an unusual amount of piety—as evidenced by her nickname of Romée, a title that indicated she had undertaken a pilgrimage to Rome at some point before getting married, probably in her teens. She gave birth to her daughter on January 6th, 1412. The baby girl was named Jeanne d'Arc.

Like most peasant children, Jeanne did not go to school—education was a privilege reserved for the wealthy and the well-born. Instead, she spent her time helping her mother around the house, learning the duties of the medieval peasant woman: cooking, cleaning, tending to animals, and gardening. One place where she did go to learn, however, was church. Europe at the time was a profoundly Catholic continent, considering that the Roman Catholic Church was the only one in existence in that area, and so little Jeanne attended mass regularly, assisted by her deeply pious mother. Here, she learned all about the saints and, most importantly, about God.

All of the information that Jeanne received about God was given to her via a priest. Unlike modern Christians, Jeanne did not learn about Him on her own by reading the Bible. Although the Bible had been fully translated into French for the first time in 1377, this did not benefit the young Jeanne much: like most peasants, she could neither read nor write. But she could listen. And listen she did, with rapt attention beside her mother in mass, as she was told about this God who had created the world and set it all in motion. She was told about Jesus, the human incarnation of God, and His death on the cross to set all sinners free. And little Jeanne was immediately in love. Following her mother's dutiful example, she threw her heart and soul into the service of God, learning her prayers and following the commandments she'd been taught.

Perhaps, even as a small child, Jeanne knew how low-born she was. She was just a little peasant child and a girl to boot—arguably the least influential person in the length and breadth of France. But she had a courage and a faith that refused to be quenched.

* * * *

Jeanne was eight years old when France finally fell. Henry V, in his quest to obtain the throne, had made his way to Troyes, and it was here that the next treaty of the Hundred Years' War was signed. King Charles VI was still deep in his insanity, lost in a strange and paranoid world where anything could happen, and his son, the Dauphin, was an unpopular figure among the French, with rumors circulating that he had ordered the murder of the Duke of Burgundy and thus placed France in the position it now found itself. Queen Isabeau of France, the wife of Charles VI, decided that something would have to be done. She herself was no favorite of the French people. They had long believed that she had had an affair with Charles VI's brother, possibly resulting in the birth of the Dauphin. Now, however, she decided that she was done with being the queen of a beleaguered country. She agreed to sign a treaty with Henry that would declare the Dauphin illegitimate and give Henry the hand of her daughter, Princess Catherine, in marriage. The Treaty of Troyes was less of a treaty and more of a French surrender. By signing it, Henry was receiving not only a princess to wed but also succession to the French throne. Charles VI would reign until his death, but if Henry and Catherine had children, they would inherit the throne of France. France was one generation away from being under English control.

The first part of the prophecy had come true. Isabeau had signed away the Dauphin's birthright, losing France to the English. It had been lost by a woman. But it would be saved by a virgin.

Chapter 3 – The First Vision

In 1425, France had two kings.

King Charles VI, the poor mad king, had died on October 21st, 1422. Not long before, his archenemy King Henry V had also passed away. Immediately, the English hurried to crown King Henry V's tiny son: a mere baby who became King Henry VI. But the Dauphin Charles, who controlled just a few territories around Bourges, also laid claim to the throne despite the treaty that had declared him illegitimate. Charles had grown up believing that he would someday be king and to have this right snatched away so cruelly by a mere babe was more than he could bear. While he was not officially crowned yet, he determined that he was the rightful king and started to tighten his grip on the central provinces of France that he still controlled. An English child may have been the official king of France, but the war raged on. Led by the Earl of Salisbury, the English army was determined to pry the last of Charles's territories out of his desperate grip. They defeated a huge French force at the Battle of Verneuil in 1424, a fight that eerily echoed the Battle of Agincourt. City after city fell, and Charles was derisively known as the "King of Bourges" since that was about all that he had under his control.

France was all but lost. Yet innocent little Jeanne d'Arc was about to experience the first event that would eventually see her transformed into the heroine of France.

* * * *

It was in 1425 that Jeanne had her first taste of what the war really meant. A thirteen-year-old girl at that point, she was poised on the threshold of adulthood, yet most of her time was occupied with ordinary household chores and simple acts of everyday piety that would not appear to be anything other than mundane. The territory surrounding Domrémy had been captured by the English army, who had gone on to fight bigger battles; Jeanne herself had seen very little of the fighting. Her father's income was stable, and as far as Jeanne was aware, the village may as well have been experiencing a time of peace.

But it did not last long. Henry of Orly, a ruthless mercenary, had a castle nearby. In these last decades of the war, neither the English nor the French were really capable of paying their soldiers; instead, most soldiers turned to pillaging the surrounding countryside in order to gain some recompense for their services. Henry was the worst of these. Loyal to no one except himself, he took advantage of a country torn by war to live a careless existence as a freebooter. He allied himself with whoever would be most advantageous to him at the time and was mostly occupied with gaining loot for himself. And one day, he decided that his next booty would be coming from Domrémy. Accompanied by his wild band of mercenaries, he descended upon the little village, sowing terror in the streets. The panicking villagers hardly knew where to flee; they expected that he would burn the houses down but remaining outside meant they would be sliced down with a sword. There was a castle nearby where they could seek shelter, but Henry came too quickly. Jeanne's peaceful little village was suddenly filled with shouting and cackling hordes of careless and dirty men, their horses' hooves clanging on the street, their swords and armor flashing in the sun. Panicking people were running in all directions. But Henry wasn't after the peasants' lives. He was after their cattle. Gathering every last piece of livestock in the village, he headed back for his castle with the lot of them, leaving the peasants alive but stripped of their means of supporting themselves and their families.

The villagers appealed to the count of Vaudemont, who quickly defeated Henry and restored the cattle to their rightful owners. Real harm was avoided, but the damage was done to the frightened peasants' psyche. Even though Vaudemont served the English, the peasants made up their minds that the war was directly responsible for the tragedy they had so nearly suffered. A common consensus was reached among them that there would be no peace and quiet until the English were driven from France once and for all.

It's likely that the prophecy was mentioned again and again in the village at this time, and that many of the villagers had hung their hopes on a lady heroine riding in on a white stallion. As for Jeanne, perhaps she hoped for the same thing. Either way, with the cattle brought back, she returned to her everyday life of doing her chores.

One of these chores was tending her father's garden. It was a strip of ground between Jeanne's house and the church where she always attended mass, and as one of the older children in the house, Jeanne was expected to tend it well. One sweltering summer day, Jeanne was hard at work in the garden. The sun was high in the sky, and sweat dripped down her young brow as she bent over the rich earth. A flash of light by the church caught her eye. She paused, rubbing her eyes, which stung with sweat. Was it just reflecting sunlight which caused the sudden burst of radiance? Yet something inside her prompted her to look again, something strangely exciting that had her a little scared. She swallowed, looking to her left, and that was when she saw him. Blinding light filled the garden, a dazzling glow that she had never seen before. Wreathed in the beams of light, she saw an angel—a towering figure, gleaming in brazen armor, with spreading wings rising up from his shoulders. He was as terrifying as he was beautiful, and Jeanne would have fled if she'd felt that she could. Instead, rooted to the spot, she just gazed up at him as his wings were thrown wide, filling her world.

She didn't have to ask the angel who he was. He was so big, so bright, and so powerful that he could only have been Michael, the archangel. He stood above her in dazzling splendor, and she could only stare. Soon, two more figures appeared beside him, both beautiful young women, and Jeanne recognized them at once. The first was Saint Catherine of Alexandria, a courageous princess who had defied the Roman Emperor Maxentius when he began to persecute Christians; Maxentius had tried everything to make her renounce her faith, from threatening the death penalty to offering to marry her, but nothing had worked. Catherine had been beheaded as a mere teenager, dying a defiant virgin, a young woman who refused to allow her faith to be broken.

The other was Saint Margaret of Antioch. Like Catherine, Margaret was a teenage martyr, the daughter of a pagan priest who promptly disowned her when she became a Christian. A Roman governor attempted to marry her, but she, too, clung to her faith and virginity. She was tortured and killed at a young age.

While it is uncertain where Jeanne could have learned about these two young women, their appearance in her first vision was something eerily prophetic. She didn't know how similar a path she was bound to walk one day. She was just a thirteen-year-old girl looking up into the faces of saints and angels in mute awe. The saints were far from the tattered teens that had been killed for their faith; now, they wore splendid, golden crowns, decked with jewels, and their faces were radiant to look upon.

Terrified, Jeanne fell to her knees. The saints hurried to reassure her that they had been sent to her by God. They went on to tell her that God had placed a high calling on her life, given her a tremendous duty to fulfill, not now but soon. He wanted her to drive the English out of France. And He wanted her to get the Dauphin to Reims and crown him king.

Then the saints were gone. Jeanne realized that she was sitting motionless in the garden, tears pouring down her cheeks. She wept not with fear but with a kind of trembling awe at the saints she had just beheld and the weight of their words to her. She didn't know why they would come to her, to little Jeanne d'Arc, an illiterate peasant girl living on the edge of France, but one thing she did know: what God told her to do, she would do.

Chapter 4 – The Doubt of Baudricourt

Over the next three years, the saints continued to visit Jeanne as she grew up in her father's house. Almost every day, the divine light would fill Jeanne's vision, and she would hear their voices telling her again that she needed to crown the Dauphin, that she was going to lead the army that would finally give France victory over the English. Every day, she grew more and more used to the saints and even began to converse with them. Yet for three years, Jeanne remained in her father's house, and she told no one.

As she was now reaching her mid-teens, Jeanne would have been considered a marriageable age. Her father, Jacques, likely was already looking around for a suitor that would be able to give Jeanne a stable and comfortable existence. But Jacques himself was about to have a dream—one that would terrify any father's heart.

One night, before Jeanne had even started to consider leaving the house, Jacques had a dream. In it, he saw his gentle and lovely daughter mounted on a horse and leaving their village with a group of rough-looking men—he knew they must be soldiers. Jacques awoke with a sweaty brow and a pounding heart. It couldn't be. Surely not his Jeanne, his sweet, pious little girl. At that moment, the prophecy was the furthest thing from Jacques's mind; Jeanne was just a peasant girl, no savior of the nation. Instead, Jacques assumed that what he'd seen in his dream was Jeanne joining the army as a prostitute. The dream was disturbing enough that he told his sons that if it ever came true, they were to drown Jeanne rather than let her sell herself in that way.

Jacques's dream would soon come true but not in the way that he thought. Jeanne was going to leave. And she was going to leave on a quest of purity and power.

* * * *

Across France, things had never looked bleaker for the disinherited Dauphin. In August 1428, the English—led primarily by the Earl of Salisbury—had landed at Calais. Joined by allies from Bedford, the English army had been swollen to a force ten thousand strong. Their intentions were clear: they were going to drive out any who dared to oppose the baby King Henry VI, claim back the territories that Charles was still clinging to, and make France an English colony once and for all.

Within a few weeks, multiple French cities had fallen before the English horde. Chartres, Janville, Meung, Beaugency, Jargeau—they didn't stand a chance. One by one they all fell at the earl's feet, and he set his sights on Orléans.

He could never have guessed how the siege of that city would end.

* * * *

In May 1428, as the French countryside was blossoming into the vivid colors of spring, Jeanne's voices started to speak to her with increasing intensity. They had long been urging her that it was time to go and meet the Dauphin, and Jeanne, seeing how ludicrous the very idea was, had been hesitating. But the voices insisted, saying that it was God's will that she needed to go and save their nation. They urged her that the Lord had chosen her for a reason. If some duke or noble was to ride forth and reclaim France, then it would be evident that the fight had been won by a man, but if a mere peasant girl like Jeanne did it, glory could only be to God. It made sense, and Jeanne finally realized that she could resist the voices no more.

She knew that the nearest garrison that remained loyal to Charles was at Vaucouleurs, a city about twelve miles from Domrémy. Once she acquiesced to her mission, her voices told her that she was to go there and appeal to Robert de Baudricourt—the captain of the garrison—for an audience with the Dauphin and safe passage to Chinon, where he was stationed at the time. Jeanne's first cousin, Durand Laxart, stayed only a few miles outside of Vaucouleurs. Telling her parents that she wanted to go and visit him, Jeanne succeeded in persuading Durand to come and pick her up at Domrémy for a visit with him and his wife, her cousin Jeanne Laxart.

During the drive, Durand could sense that there was something different about young Jeanne. Something had changed in the bright blue of her eyes; there was a presence about her, a glow that he couldn't quite place. He didn't ask, however, concentrating on the road instead as his horse took them briskly toward home. At last—it is uncertain whether this happened during the drive or in Durand's home—Jeanne opened up, talking about her visions for the first time. Gathering her courage, she told Durand that she needed to go "into France" (referring to central France, the area still governed by the Dauphin).

"Why?" her first cousin inquired, knowing that central France was a war zone.

"I need to crown the Dauphin at Reims," Jeanne answered calmly.

Durand stared at her, wondering if she knew how ridiculous her words were. But those blue eyes remained as serene as still pools of deep water as she studied him, her voice steady and sure. "Has it not been said," she added, "that France would be ruined by a woman and later restored by a virgin?"

Durand didn't know what to say. He knew as well as any Frenchman that Isabeau had signed away her own country, and he had heard the prophecy over and over again. Yet he had never imagined that this virgin savior could come from a place like Domrémy, that it could be a peasant girl, that it could be *this* little peasant girl, his own cousin Jeanne d'Arc.

She went on to tell him that she had to get to Vaucouleurs and to Robert de Baudricourt. And perhaps it was the fire in her eyes or perhaps it was the desperation in Durand's own heart, but he decided that he believed her. He vowed that he would take her to Vaucouleurs and get her that audience with the captain, no matter how crazy it would make him look.

* * * *

Robert de Baudricourt was captain of the small garrison at Vaucouleurs. Itself a small town, Vaucouleurs was so familiar to the twenty-eight-year-old captain that he knew almost every face in it. He certainly recognized Durand Laxart, but as for the girl following him, she was a stranger to him. There was something ethereal about her as she approached. She wore a torn, tattered red dress, a faded thing that had been mended often; her body was slender, her features pinched, but those eyes. They were an almost indefinable shade of blue, and the light inside them made Robert stare for a few moments as Durand walked past. When the girl's eyes rested on him, she stopped, her face lighting up in recognition even though Robert knew he had never seen her before. She grabbed Durand's arm and pointed, and they made their way up to Robert.

Durand introduced Jeanne as his cousin who was staying with him for a while. Bemused, Robert asked her what she wanted, expecting her to have some foolish request that he could easily push aside. Instead, the girl spoke with a clarity and a strength that he had not been expecting.

"I have come to you on the part of my Lord," she told him, "in order that you may send word to the Dauphin, to hold fast, and to not cease war against his enemies."

Robert blinked. He was only a minor noble, one who had likely never actually exchanged a single word with the Dauphin, let alone told him what to do. Before he could demand who this Jeanne thought she was—or who she thought *he* was to have that kind of authority—she went on. "Before mid-Lent, the Lord will give him help," she told him. "In truth, the kingdom belongs not to the Dauphin but to my Lord."

Angered, Robert glared at her. He was one of the last Dauphin loyalists left in one of the last cities in the area that would still dare to voice its alliance to him instead of submitting to the Anglo-Burgundians. He was about to rebuke her for assuming that anyone other than the Dauphin Charles could be made king when she interrupted. "But my Lord wills that the Dauphin be made king and have the kingdom in [his] command. Notwithstanding his enemies, the Dauphin will be made king." She raised her chin, her eyes filled with something that was nothing like pride but as sure as steel. "And it is I that will conduct him to the coronation."

It was all that Robert could do not to burst out laughing. This raggedy peasant girl seemed to truly believe that she was going to crown the Dauphin, despite the fact that she could never even behold his face with her low-born status. "And who is this Lord of yours?" he demanded.

"God," Jeanne replied simply.

Robert shook his head with a derisive snort. Turning to Durand, he said, "Take this girl back to her father and box her ears." Then he dismissed them with a flick of his hand.

* * * *

Jeanne was immediately dismayed by Robert's reaction to her request. Subdued, she asked Durand to take her back home to her father. Heartbroken for his cousin's unhappiness, awed by her ability to somehow recognize Robert even though she had never seen him before, and upset at Robert's reaction, Durand dutifully drove her back home to Domrémy.

That could have been the last that anyone ever heard of Jeanne d'Arc. But things were about to take a turn for the worse in the war and in everyday life in Domrémy—a turn that would inspire Jeanne to go back to Vaucouleurs. And this time, she would have help.

Chapter 5 – A Prediction of Defeat

15th-century Orléans
https://commons.wikimedia.org/wiki/File:View_of_Orl%C3%A9ans_1428_-_Project_Gutenberg_etext_19488.jpg

After conquering Meung on September 8th, 1428, the Earl of Salisbury knew that he was ready to press home his advantage. There was one last major obstacle standing between him and central France which was controlled by the Dauphin. That obstacle was the Loire River, and it was guarded by the city of Orléans. Also at the time the capital of the duchy of Orléans, it was of political as well as strategic importance. Taking it down would be breaking apart the last wall that stood between the English and the heart of France, and if Orléans fell, the Dauphin's claim to the throne would be all but lost.

The city itself was built on the northern shore of the Loire, and the only way to access it was via a bridge guarded by a gatehouse named Les Tourelles. It was at the Tourelles that the Earl of Salisbury mounted his first attack on October 12th, 1428. The Siege of Orléans had begun. And if that city fell, France would be doomed.

* * * *

Just before the siege began, Jeanne had started feeling the effects of the war once again.

A few weeks after her return to Domrémy, the English and Burgundians decided that Vaucouleurs, in its puny defiance, was a thorn in the side that they would no longer tolerate. It may have been a small town, but it was a loyal one to the Dauphin, and it was time to beat its inhabitants—and those of the surrounding villagers—into submission. The first warning that Jeanne had was the deafening ringing of the church bell next door to her home. Its sound, normally so melodious, was now a cacophonous clang as the bell-ringer pulled desperately at the rope, pealing a loud warning through the streets of Domrémy. The d'Arc family had no choice but to flee. Taking Jeanne with them, they had to drive their cattle across open territory to the fortified Neufchâteau, where they were forced to seek shelter in an inn.

When the army was gone, Jeanne and her family returned to a ruined Domrémy. Fields and houses were damaged by fire and wanton destruction. The English had not cared how peace-loving the peasants of Domrémy were; they belonged to the French, and thus they were enemies, no matter how uninvolved they really were in the war. Worst of all, they had burned the church. The sight broke Jeanne's heart. Her saints had never stopped urging her to get back to Vaucouleurs and find her way to the Dauphin, and as soon as the fighting in the immediate vicinity was over, that was exactly what she did.

* * * *

There was something final about Jeanne's second departure from the village where she'd grown up. Her heart was torn to leave her parents and still more torn by the untruth she told them—that she was leaving in order to act as a nurse and helper for Jeanne Laxart, who was expecting a baby. In truth, part of Jeanne's soul knew that she would never see idyllic Domrémy again. She watched it fade into the distance, its quaint little church, its snowbound fields, its beautiful wood, the garden where she'd first heard the voices, and knew in her heart of hearts that she would never go back.

It was January 1429. The Siege of Orléans had been raging for three months, and there was still no end in sight. French reinforcements had been able to squeeze through the English lines here and there, enabling the city to hang on far longer than expected. The death of the Earl of Salisbury had been a setback for England, but he was replaced by the Earl of Suffolk, and the siege continued undeterred. For months, small skirmishes had been sparking all over the city, but it was generally at something of a stalemate, with the French stubbornly holding on within the walls and the English firmly dug in outside them. All of central France hung in nervous limbo, with the might of the English encamped only about seventy-five miles from the administrative capital of Bourges.

Jeanne didn't know much about the details. Rumors among the peasants would likely have told her that a siege had been laid to Orléans, but apart from this, no one would have given an ignorant little peasant much information. She knew that the voices were urging her more and more intensely to go back to Vaucouleurs, and that was enough for her.

Arriving at Vaucouleurs, Jeanne lodged with the Leroyer family, where she worked as a servant to Henri and Catherine Leroyer. It was here that she first really caught the eye of Jean de Metz. One of Robert's squires, Jean had been present during her first meeting with Robert, and something about the girl's glittering presence inspired him. When he spotted her heading toward the garrison once more, he knew he had to speak to her.

Approaching her, he hoped she would recognize him from her first meeting with Baudricourt. "What are you doing here, my friend?" he asked. Suddenly nervous faced with her innocent blue eyes, Jean fumbled, trying to make some small talk. The war was the first thing that came to mind; it had been going on for so many decades that talking about the war was like talking about the weather. "Must the King be driven from the kingdom?" he said conversationally. "And are we to be English?"

Jeanne studied him for a few seconds. Her eyes were completely serene as she spoke. "I am come here to this royal town to speak to Robert de Baudricourt," she said.

Jean was not surprised. He had known, despite the defeat in her eyes the last time she met with his master, that Jeanne would not give up so easily. She went on to explain again that she needed Robert to take her to the king but that he hadn't taken her or her words seriously. "Nevertheless, before the middle of Lent, I must be with the King," she said. "There is no succor to be expected save from me."

The quiet confidence in her words took Jean by surprise. He studied her, wondering how this work-worn peasant girl could possibly have come to this conclusion. She added that she would rather have stayed home, spinning wool with her mother, but that she had to go to the King "because my Lord wills that I should do it."

The way she said the Lord's name rang with authority. Looking at her bearing, at the complete lack of arrogance in the way she held herself, and in the utter conviction in her tone, Jean knew she was speaking the truth. Somehow, God had chosen this girl, this piece of nothing in the face of a haughty society, to save the nation of France from the marauding English. He reached out, taking her small hand in his. It was rough and hard from manual labor. "With God's guidance, I promise, I will conduct you to the King," he said.

* * * *

Between Jean and another knight and fellow supporter of Jeanne, Bertrand de Poulengy, they succeeded in securing another audience with Robert for her. Dubious though Robert was, he couldn't seem to forget the light in the eyes of the young girl with her crazy claims that had visited him last spring. Now she was back, here in the crispness of February 12th, 1429, and Robert was getting desperate. Vaucouleurs had suffered during the war, Orléans was besieged, and France was all but lost. It couldn't hurt to hear out this little lunatic.

Upon meeting with Robert, Jeanne told him, again, what she wanted from him: to be taken safely through enemy territory to meet with the Dauphin. Then she added that the Dauphin's forces were about to suffer a terrible defeat.

As Jeanne spoke to Robert, hundreds of miles away on a great flat plain near Rouvray, there was the crack of gunpowder and the whine of cannonballs launching through the air. 1,600 Englishmen dived for cover as cannonballs punched into their wagon train. It had been drawn into a makeshift defensive formation, with sharpened spikes plunged into the earth around the wagon train in a bid to hold off the French, but the English were well aware that there were twice as many men in the attacking Franco-Scottish army as in this baggage train. Wagons splintered, supplies spilling out onto the ground: barrels of herring, stacks of artillery. Hope leaped in the hearts of the French army. If they could stop this baggage train from reaching Orléans, the siege might just be over.

"What?" Robert stared at the girl. "What do you mean?"

"The Dauphin's arms have this day suffered a great reverse near Orléans," Jeanne repeated.

It was madness, Robert thought. Yet the calm conviction in her eyes chilled him to the core.

There was a shout of dismay from the French. The Scottish part of their army was charging, overexcited by the damage the cannons had inflicted on the English. The French had to cease fire, and the English rose, firing with crossbows and longbows from behind their wagons. The Scottish ranks crumbled, men dying in all directions. The French were forced to lead a cavalry charge that they knew would be ineffective against the English archers. They were right. In minutes, the English led a counterattack, and the French and Scottish were ignominiously routed.

"Get out," Robert ordered Jeanne. "Go."

* * * *

A few days later, the news reached Vaucouleurs. The Franco-Scottish army had tried to stop a baggage train from reaching Orléans and horribly failed, losing about six hundred men, while the English lost only four. It was a humiliating defeat, since known as the Battle of the Herrings.

When Robert heard the news, and heard that the fight had taken place on the same day as his meeting with Jeanne, he knew that her prediction had been true. And if that was true, maybe it was also true that she was the savior of France.

He called her to his garrison and told her that he would send her to Chinon with Jean and Bertrand. His words were those of a desperate man, still doubting but unable to find any other shred of hope to cling to. "Go," he told her. "And let come what may."

Chapter 6 – An Audience with the King

The road to Chinon was fraught with danger. Charles's court was about three hundred miles away from Vaucouleurs, a distance that would take at least a week of hard riding, but that was the least of Jean's and Bertrand's worries as they considered how best to escort their young and innocent charge to the court of the Dauphin. The truth was that Vaucouleurs and its surrounding villages were some of the most isolated territories remaining under French control. To reach Chinon, they would have to cross a vast expanse of enemy territory, effectively trespassing on the lands of the infant English king. Somehow they had to get to Chinon without attracting enemy attention, which would have been hard enough for a group of men, let alone only a few knights guarding a vulnerable young woman who had no experience of war and—it seemed—little comprehension of danger.

Together with the people of Vaucouleurs, who had noticed Jeanne's repeated visits to Robert and learned via rumors of her quest, Jean and Bertrand decided that the safest way to get Jeanne to

Chinon would be to disguise her as a man. Jeanne willingly agreed with the idea, despite the fact that cross-dressing was widely considered to be a heinous crime in that era; however, Jeanne and everyone she spoke to thought of it as a normal and necessary precaution against attack from those who might want to carry her off and have their way with her. Luckily for Jeanne, she had become something of a sensation in Vaucouleurs. Long known as a virtuous and kind girl—albeit a little odd—she had suddenly become the hope of the hopeless. The mere fact that Robert was willing to send her to Chinon at all gave her credibility in the eyes of the people. They believed that she was going to save them and the rest of their nation from the English, and they would do anything for her. Making her some suitable clothing for the journey was the least they could do.

While this was being undertaken, Jean headed off and bought a horse. The people of Vaucouleurs presented Jeanne with a sword as well as the clothing, and she was well disguised as a fellow knight when she set off with her small retinue: Jean, Bertrand, and two other men-at-arms. Bertrand paid for the journey. They left Vaucouleurs on February 23rd, 1429, beginning their perilous journey through an area that was controlled by the Burgundians at the time.

For ten days, Jeanne and her companions rode by night and slept by day, using little lanes and forgotten roadways to avoid detection by their enemies. It must have been a strange and new experience for the innocent young Jeanne, riding a strong and lively horse in between a group of rough soldiers. It's unlikely that she had ever ridden much considering her family's lowly status; she would also have never worn anything like the hosen (tight pants) that she found herself in now. Everything would have been new and uncomfortable for her, and she was traveling more in a day than she ever had in her entire life. Yet her two guardians would later testify that she remained her sweet, gentle self. Not a single curse passed her lips, nor did she conduct herself with anything other than calm confidence. Even the seasoned warriors were fearing for their lives as they traversed the dangerous landscape, but Jeanne showed no fear. She told them that it was God's will for them to get to Chinon, and get to Chinon they would.

Jeanne also owed much of her safety to the two knights who so fervently believed in her. They never left her side. At night, she slept safely between the two of them, who would rather have cut off their own heads than lay a finger on the young maiden lying so close.

The only thing that really troubled Jeanne during the journey was that she wanted to go to Mass. As the churches were occupied by the English and there was some risk that the French knights would have been identified, this was impossible.

Finally, on March 6th, 1429, they reached Chinon at last, utterly unharmed. The perilous journey was over. But now, Jeanne had to do more than convince a lowly captain of the guard to grant her passage to Chinon. She had to get herself an audience with the Dauphin himself.

* * * *

The Dauphin Charles was a desperate man. Despite being only twenty-six years old, he had had everything taken from him. Having grown up in a household with a mentally ill father whose rampages were, by turns, humiliating and dangerous, Charles's great hope had been the knowledge that he would someday be king—a better king by far than his mad predecessor.

Then came the terrible blow dealt to him by his own mother, Isabeau. Supporting the rumors that said that Charles was an illegitimate product of an affair between Isabeau and his uncle Louis, she signed away her own son's birthright to his greatest enemy. The bitterness of it was terrible, and Charles was aware that despite the fact that he saw himself as the rightful king of France, he had little hope of ever claiming his throne. The English were at his very threshold. It would not be long before his army fell and his country belonged to some English baby.

In fact, Charles had all but given up hope. He hung around in Chinon now, watching the progress of the war with a numbed sense of inevitable defeat. He was doomed. He always had been.

He was in this state when one of his courtiers came to inform him that a strange young woman had just arrived in Chinon; a mere peasant girl, dressed as a young man, bearing a sword and astride a horse. Her name, the courtier told him, was Jeanne d'Arc. She said that she was going to save the nation of France. She said that God had sent her.

At first, Charles wanted to laugh. But somehow, the idea sparked a flicker of interest in him. He had nothing left to lose—everything had been stripped from him. Hearing this girl out was a desperate measure, but he was a desperate man. She would have to prove, however, that she really did have divine help. He decided that he was going to dress as an ordinary courtier and then have Jeanne brought into a room full of similarly dressed men. If she could identify him, he would grant her a personal audience. This was an age before photographs; in wartime France, some peasant girl from hundreds of miles away would have no idea what the Dauphin looked like.

All was done as Charles ordered. The courtiers were all gathered together, slightly unnerved by seeing their Dauphin dressed like them, and another courtier was told to pretend to be the king once Jeanne had made her selection. Faintly bored and apathetic, Charles waited for the appearance of this girl who said that the saints were talking to her.

The doors opened, and Jeanne was shown in. Charles was struck by her at once. Her hair had been roughly cut short, but there was no hiding her willowy figure, her glittering eyes. There was something about her that commanded his attention, and all eyes were on the girl as she walked into the room, her eyes wandering along the lines of courtiers. She seemed focused inward somehow, as if listening to something that only she could hear. A faint smile played on her lips as she gazed from face to face. When her eyes lit on Charles, the incredible happened. Her eyes widened in recognition, and she rushed up to him, her eyes locked on his for a breathtaking moment. Then she fell to her knees, throwing her arms around his legs. Their grip held the strength of a girl who had spent her life working. "God give you a happy life, sweet King!" she cried out.

Charles was stunned, but he managed to keep it together. Pulling away from her, he chided her, telling her that he was no king. Shaken though he was, the courtier that had been designated to play the role of the Dauphin stepped forward, saying that he was the king of France. But Jeanne would not be fooled. She continued to stay close to Charles, repeating over and over that he was the king, that her voices had told her so.

Awestruck, Charles gladly did what he had agreed to do: he granted her a private audience. Maybe, just maybe, the God that he felt had abandoned him for his entire life had finally decided to have mercy—and if He chose to do so through this random little peasant girl, Charles, royal though he was, was in no position to argue.

Chapter 7 – The Road to Orléans

Jeanne with her armor and famous banner
https://commons.wikimedia.org/wiki/File:Portrait_jeanne_d%27arc.jpg

The details of Charles's private audience with Jeanne have never really been known to anyone, except for Charles and Jeanne themselves. Some sources say that Jeanne told him about a private prayer, something intensely personal and a secret that he had never shared with anyone. According to some, this prayer involved Charles's claim to the throne, but in it, the defeated Dauphin did not petition the Lord to bring him to the throne. Instead, in paralyzing insecurity, Charles begged God to punish himself alone instead of all the people if he truly was an illegitimate heir. The question had been plaguing him for years. He had no idea if he really was the product of a lawful union between the king and queen; perhaps he was illegitimate after all, the result of a cheating queen and a deceitful brother. Yet he couldn't tell his people that even he doubted his own legitimacy. He could only tell this to God, and he did so in a heartfelt prayer, pouring out his fear and agony in private.

Except Jeanne knew. She told him all about it, and she assured him that he was the rightful king, that it was the blood of Charles the Mad in his veins after all, and that it was God's will for him to ascend to the throne.

This is all speculation, however. Jeanne herself was tight-lipped for the rest of her life about this meeting, refusing to reveal any confidential details. Yet one thing is absolutely for certain: Jeanne made an impression on the Dauphin that left little doubt in his mind that God really had sent her, and that she really had the potential to save France from its overwhelming enemy.

The Dauphin's advisers were not as easily convinced, despite the fact that after his meeting with Jeanne, Charles was a changed man. Whatever she had said to him, it left him radiant, glowing with a new courage and conviction that they knew promised to be beneficial to the people who were desperate for a brave and motivated leader. However, they knew that caution had to be exercised. If Jeanne turned out to be some witch or heretic, the entire question of Charles's legitimacy would once again be raised even if he was able to get his throne back.

On their advice, Charles decided that Jeanne would be sent to Poitiers—the last theological establishment still within the Dauphin's control—to be thoroughly examined. She arrived there on March 11th, 1429, only a few days after her audience with the Dauphin, and stayed with Charles's advocate in Parliament. Some of the leading theologians left in France were there to conduct the examination, including doctors in theology, abbots, bishops, and several councilors who were educated in law. If there was a blemish on Jeanne's character or a reason to doubt her faith, these people would find it.

And so, a simple, illiterate farm girl from Domrémy found herself the subject of fierce scrutiny by some of the most educated men in the country. As much as France was desperate for a hero—or heroine, as it seemed—these men were determined to thoroughly prove if she was telling the truth. They knew that she was uneducated, that she was, to all accounts, a mere nobody, and they knew that the implications of sending her to the front and then seeing her fail would be enormous. She could be the last piece of hope the French had, and if that hope turned out to be false, morale would plummet and the war would be lost already. The theologians decided to show her no mercy and take no prisoners, simple though she might have seemed to be.

It was quickly evident that, as sweet as Jeanne was, she was no fool, nor was she even remotely intimidated by the important men who were questioning her. She firmly believed that the God of Heaven was on her side, and compared to Him, the theologians were nothing. They quickly started to question her about the voices she heard, trying to establish if they were saints or simply figments of an insane mind. One of the first questions, asked by Brother Seguin de Seguin, a professor of theology, was about the dialect that the saints spoke to her. "A better one than you," Jeanne answered with fierce calm.

Taken aback and yet somehow charmed by her fearlessness, Seguin looked her directly in the eyes and asked the simplest question of all. "Do you believe in God?"

Those bright blue eyes seemed to be staring directly into his soul. "In truth," she responded, "more than yourself!"

Seguin was surprised by her answer but impressed by the way in which she said it. There was no pride in her, only a sturdy assurance that he couldn't seem to find his way around. He told her that as much as she may believe in God, she couldn't prove that He had really sent her unless she gave the court some kind of a sign—a miracle from above to prove that what she told them was true. Throughout the interrogation, Jeanne had been asserting that she was going to break the siege at Orléans and crown Charles at Reims. When Seguin asked for a sign, Jeanne folded her arms in defiance. "I am not come to Poitiers to show signs," she retorted. "Send me to Orléans, where I shall show you the signs by which I am sent."

For the next three weeks, Jeanne was not only questioned in the chapel at Poitiers, but she was also followed and watched in secret, as it was determined that her private life had to be impeccable as well for her to be deemed worthy of the hope that the people were so eager to place upon her shoulders. Yet both in the interrogation and in their surveillance of her daily activities, the theologians could find no fault in her. In April 1429, they sent word to the Dauphin. The fact that Jeanne was a fervent Christian, upstanding in every moral way and as devoted in her faith as she was courageous, was indisputable; but whether or not she really was going to be able to lift the siege as she promised, they couldn't say, although they considered it likely. Their suggestion was to send her to Orléans, and if she perished, then she perished. If she won the battle, then so much the better. The Dauphin was to send her there as a test, as she had requested.

* * * *

During Jeanne's examination in Poitiers, a relief expedition was being planned to go to Orléans in a bid to free the beleaguered city from the English. Once her examination was over, Jeanne saw the expedition as an ideal opportunity to make her way to Orléans. Considering that she'd passed the test with flying colors, Charles had little choice other than to allow her to go—although it is likely that he was not reluctant to send her there, believing, as many of the French people did, that Jeanne was the heroine they'd been waiting for. The Maiden that all the prophecies had foretold.

It didn't take long for her newfound credibility to reach the ears of the rich and noble, either. They pulled together to donate everything that Jeanne needed, pouring their money into this new hope. A suit of armor was created specifically for her in order to fit her feminine curves; she was given a sword and a shining white stallion, and finally, a banner. This banner was a simple thing—a depiction of Jesus, holding the world in His hands, flanked by two angels on a white background—but it would soon become the most powerful weapon in the Hundred Years' War. For while it would shed no blood, the whole army of France would rally behind it.

Chapter 8 – Arrival at Orléans

The French soldiers knew that they were on the brink of defeat.

They had been trapped inside Orléans for almost six months, watching the English fortifications grow, aware that with every passing day their enemies were mining underneath the French defenses, pushing their fortifications slowly nearer and nearer to the city walls. Worse, for five long months, only a handful of supply convoys had been able to make it through to the city. The English might not have been able to fully surround Orléans, but they had enough forces that any convoy approaching it had to take a long roundabout route through enemy territory, resulting in many convoys being discovered and captured. The English knew that they didn't have enough men to win the battle by direct assault. So, they decided to starve it to death instead.

It was working. Five months of hunger were taking their toll on the soldiers' morale. The fact that the English convoys were making it through—even when opposed by a significantly larger army, as demonstrated in the Battle of Herrings—didn't help. Soldiers and citizens of the city alike had to watch as the English feasted happily in their trenches, while inside Orléans, people went to bed on empty stomachs.

Rumors were circulating around the city that Orléans was on the brink of surrender, further causing morale to plummet. In fact, Orléans had already made an offer of surrender to Duke Philip III of Burgundy, and it was an offer that he found very attractive. Not only would control over the city allow his English allies to continue their campaign into central France, but half of its taxes would go to Burgundy as well, and Burgundy would be allowed to appoint its governors. In early April, Philip hurried to Paris, asking the English regent—the Duke of Bedford—to lift the siege so that Philip could accept the terms of surrender.

The Duke of Bedford refused absolutely. He was delighted by the news of this proposal, knowing that it meant Orléans had been brought to its knees. All that was left now was to deliver the *coup de grace*. Surely, in only a few weeks, Orléans would fall. According to medieval law and tradition, the citizens of a city that had resisted a siege (and no city had resisted more strenuously than Orléans) could be killed by an invading army once they had entered. It would be a bloodbath, and whatever citizens of Orléans were left would be slaves of the English. Bedford's control over Orléans would be absolute, and he was confident that it was only a matter of time before the city fell once and for all.

The situation was so dire for France that the Dauphin Charles's advisers were telling him that the French throne was a lost cause. Abdicating and fleeing to Scotland was the only option that would allow him to lead a peaceful and relatively free life; death or capture awaited should he continue to pursue the crown that was his birthright. But Charles refused to listen. A new hope had been awakened in him. And that hope was on its way to Orléans, dressed in a special suit of armor, riding a white stallion, and holding a white banner.

* * * *

Whispers of this mysterious girl had been flying through Orléans for almost two months. She was a virgin, they all said, a young girl from the borders of Lorraine who had been to see the Dauphin, and made such an impression on him that she was at that very moment on her way to Orléans with a much-needed relief expedition. And did not the prophecy say that such a girl would be the one to save the nation of France? It was the only piece of hope that the French soldiers had left, and they clung to it fiercely.

When news came that the relief expedition had almost reached Orléans and that one of its key commanders, Jean de Dunois, had headed out to meet it, excitement filled the hearts of the waiting soldiers. Men-at-arms and civilians alike started to gather in the streets, a murmur of excitement running through the crowd. Could it be true? Was she really here? Had God really sent her, as she'd told the Dauphin? They said that they had tested her at Poitiers and she had passed the test. Were they about to be saved?

More whispers filled the streets. The boats had gone out across the Loire to meet the relief expedition a few miles east of Orléans. When this mysterious maiden had gotten into the boat, the wind had magically changed, and they were sailing swiftly and under cover of darkness back to the city. It was a miracle, they were saying, though many doubted that the story was true. Yet even they had to hope that she had help from above.

Then they saw her. They saw the banner first, waving above the heads of the crowd, a shining white flag that waved in the breeze. Then she emerged, riding down the streets on a white charger that champed and snorted and pulled at the bit, yet this small and wispy young girl seemed to control him with ease. She wore a suit of plate armor and a wide-eyed smile, and when they looked into her bright blue eyes, they saw nothing but an unshakable confidence. It was something to believe in, and it threw the whole city of Orléans into rejoicing. They were cheering, dancing in the streets, praying out loud, praising God, chanting her name: *Jeanne d'Arc. Jeanne d'Arc.*

* * * *

Jeanne had not been idle during her journey to Orléans. Meeting her small army at Blois, she had proceeded to dictate a letter to the English, giving them a chance to flee from France before she and her army attacked. Her statements were as forceful as they were simple, asserting that God wanted the Dauphin Charles to be on the throne of France and that the English were to be gone — "Or I will make you go," she concluded. She signed her letter, simply, *La Pucelle*—The Maiden.

Of course, the English jeered at Jeanne's letters. Who was this simpleton, this mere peasant girl, to tell them to go, let alone somehow "make" them leave? They continued to insult and deprecate Jeanne when she was in Orléans, and she continued to send messengers to them demanding their retreat. The English were having none of it. They knew Orléans was on the edge of defeat, and they believed that their faith in this mad young girl was just another sign of their impending downfall. They called her a witch and a lunatic. It was on their lips that her name would first be spoken in English, a name that has gone down in history: Joan of Arc.

Joan didn't let any amount of English stubbornness deter her. When the English refused to back down, she ordered a charge against them. Jean de Dunois immediately put a stop to this, protesting that the garrison was too small to launch an offensive on the English—he would have to ride to Blois for still more reinforcements before this would be possible. On May 1st, he left the city, sneaking out to Blois. With his stern presence gone, Joan was free to do more or less whatever she wanted. She rode out of the city and inspected the English fortifications to the bemusement of the English warriors. They shouted various slurs at her from their fortifications but didn't attack her. After all, what did she know of battles? What damage could she possibly do? What threat could she possibly be?

Chapter 9 – Flying the White Banner

Joan and her banner at the Siege of Orléans
https://commons.wikimedia.org/wiki/File:Lenepveu,_Jeanne_d%27Arc_au_si%C3%A8ge_d%27Orl%C3%A9ans.jpg

Among the French army, Joan was rapidly gaining popularity. Now that more soldiers had actually set eyes on her, she was being called the Maid of France, the virgin savior who had been in the prophecies for so many years. The response was tremendous. French morale, which had been plundered by almost a century of war, suddenly began to climb. Deserters returned to the army, and suddenly, every brave young nobleman in France wanted to join up and strike a blow for the Dauphin because word had it that there was a saint at the front, that God was on their side. When Joan rode through the streets, she had to have an escort of knights with her or the exuberant crowd would snatch her right from her saddle in their excitement. They lined the streets everywhere she went, gazing at her in awe.

On May 4th, Dunois returned, bringing with him the suddenly swollen ranks of the bulk of the French army. He was surprised to see the sheer number of men that had either returned or joined thanks to the presence of Joan at Orléans. Joan rode out to meet the approaching army with a small group of men in case of attack, but despite the fact that the English were within sight, the army made it safely to Orléans. Joan and Dunois had dinner together that evening, and Dunois promised that he would send Joan's page boy to her with news if any combat took place.

However, it appears that Joan's page failed in his duties. That very night, Dunois and a group of 1,500 men launched an assault on an English bastille named St. Loup, and Joan was fast asleep when this took place. Suddenly, she woke and rushed to shake her attendant awake. Joan's words and thoughts were still vague and sluggish with sleep, but her message was urgent: her voices had told her that she had to go to battle. Rushing to scold her page for his misbehavior, Joan ordered him to fetch her horse while other attendants helped her into her armor. In a flurry of activity, Joan jumped onto her white stallion, seized her banner, and then set spurs to her horse, sending him galloping madly out of the city.

Followed by some of her companions, Joan rode toward St. Loup, and it was here that she witnessed what real battle was for the first time. For a gentle peasant girl, it would have been a horrible shock. Even though she had had to flee from the English before, never had she seen death and destruction on such a terrifying scale. Tears ran down her cheeks as she beheld the wounded being carried back to Orléans; worse still were the torn and gutted bodies of the soldiers who had lost their lives in the fight. They were scattered carelessly across the battlefield, their blood soaking into the earth, flies buzzing around their motionless limbs and walking across their glazed and staring eyes. Skin was torn aside, splintered bone brutally exposed, and innards were ripped and spilling from bloated bodies. This was battle, and it was real, with real blood on the dirt, the real stench of death in the air, and real people losing their lives.

As real as the fight was, Joan's faith was more real still. Ashen-faced and crying, Joan did not allow the horrific sight to stop her. She spurred her horse on and rode for St. Loup. Despite the fact that the French outnumbered the English garrison there more than three to one, they were struggling, facing yet another disheartening defeat until they heard a pure young voice cry out from the direction of Orléans. It was Joan. When the French saw her banner snapping above her head, its whiteness stark against the blue sky, they rallied. Petrified of the "witch," the English faltered. The French surged forward, pushing the English back to the bell tower of the fort, and within a few hours, the English had fallen. St. Loup was in French hands, and Joan's first victory had been won.

Although more than 100 Englishmen died, and even though Joan wore a sword, no one was struck down by her personally. Instead, she seemed deeply grieved by their deaths, even though she had deemed them necessary. She wept over their bodies, wishing that they had just heeded the warnings she'd given them in the name of God. But much more blood would be shed, and this innocent girl would see much more death and gore before Orléans would finally be set free.

* * * *

The victory at St. Loup was just the beginning, the first taste of success for which the French army had been so desperate. The next day, May 5th, was Ascension Day; they celebrated the feast day in rest, but Joan took the opportunity to dictate one last letter to the English. Tying it to an arrow, it was shot into the English ranks. Their response was so derisive and so badly insulted Joan's purity and character that it brought her to tears, but it did not stop her.

On May 6th, the fighting began again as the French gathered themselves to begin an assault in earnest. The eventual goal was simple: to recapture Les Tourelles, the gatehouse that the English had been controlling since the fateful beginning of the siege. To do this, they first had to destroy several English bastilles, such as Boulevart, Augustins, and St. Privé. When the day dawned, the military commanders were aghast to find that the civilians of Orléans had rallied around the white banner of their heroine and formed a makeshift militia that was rich in passion but lamentably low in equipment and training. Nonetheless, Joan persuaded the commanders to let the people join in, and so they sailed across the Loire together, Joan's white stallion being ferried over the river on a boat. The white horse's hooves had barely struck the shore before Joan was swinging its head toward the bastille of Boulevart, shouting for her troops to rally around her. They would have followed her anywhere, and so when she charged Boulevart, to the dismay of the commanders, her people went with her. The move, probably precipitated by one of Joan's voices, was unplanned and dangerous. Charging upon Boulevart, they began to assault the bastille, but their passion quickly faded when cries of dismay were heard. The English were sending reinforcements to Boulevart from St. Privé. Terror seized the French, and they began to fall back, physically pulling Joan's horse with them. What happened next is uncertain, but the only version that legend and history gives us is that the English troops burst out of the bastille to give chase. When Joan saw them coming, she wrenched her horse back around and raised her banner aloft, shouting four words that became her motto, her battle cry, and her personal anthem: *Au Nom de Dieu!* ("In the Name of God!"). She stood alone, her own people fleeing, her enemy charging, and she shouted the words that she believed in, holding up her flag as a symbol of hope and courage. The English, suddenly disconcerted by this turn of events, skidded to a halt. The French rallied, and the assault began afresh.

This time, it was successful. By the end of the day, St. Privé had been evacuated, Boulevart had fallen, and Les Augustins was in the hands of the French. They had torn down every obstacle that stood between them and Les Tourelles. Now it was time to take back their city.

Chapter 10 – A Sign Provided

May 7th, 1429 dawned with hope. The French had made more progress in a single day than they had since the beginning of the siege many months ago. Les Tourelles was within their sight, almost within their grasp. Thanks to the strange young peasant girl, erratic as her actions could be, they were starting to believe that perhaps the siege could be lifted after all.

Joan had proven herself courageous, but she had also been unpredictable, and her wild presence made some of the commanders uncomfortable. What was more, she had obtained a fairly minor but still painful wound in her foot during the fight at Les Augustins, and so the commanders tried to persuade her to stay in Orléans for the final assault. Perhaps Joan considered doing as they asked. She had been in the thick of the fight that day, a fight for which she had received no training or conditioning; she had experienced the mass destruction and thoughtless carnage of real war and even felt what it was like to be injured in it. It was all suddenly very real. Yet even this could not persuade Joan to change any of her convictions: she believed God had told her to lift the siege, and lift it she would, no matter what.

That night, she told one of her close associates, Jean Pasquerel, a friar who served as her confessor, to stay close to her, "for tomorrow I will have much to do and more than I ever had, and tomorrow blood will leave my body above my breast." This ominous prediction didn't seem to have much effect on Joan's determination to join in the coming battle.

The next morning, as the day broke, the French rushed forth. They poured toward the gates of Les Tourelles, bright and swift as the beams of sunlight gushing over the landscape as the sun rose, and it seemed that nothing could stop them; one history describes the zeal of the French soldiers as so powerful that they seemed to "believe themselves immortal." Their eyes fixed on Joan's white banner as she rode out before them, and they launched themselves at Les Tourelles, where they bombarded their enemies for hours upon hours. Cannons cracked, swords clashed, voices screamed, and above it all, the serene white banner of Joan of Arc floated upon the breeze. She was always in the thick of it yet never striking a blow. She didn't need to. Her mere presence, the assurance in her blue eyes, and the rise and fall of her lilting voice calling out her war cry of *Au Nom de Dieu!* was stronger than the sharpest two-edged sword, more powerful than the biggest cannon.

The morning wore on with the French fighting on with strength and perseverance. Their courage somehow found no end, their endurance unabated as their beloved Joan stayed shoulder-to-shoulder with them, crying out encouragements. She would not strike a blow, but she was a weapon in and of herself.

As the sun began to reach its zenith, it happened. The ominous prophecy Joan had made about herself came suddenly and sickeningly true. Jean Pasquerel, as Joan had asked, was right next to her when he heard the twang of an English bowstring. Joan, halfway through helping to prop up a scaling ladder against the wall of the fortress, barely had time to look up before the arrow hit her. The force of it flung her off her feet, cruelly smashing her tiny body against the earth with a dull thud and the ring of armor. Blood spilled upon the ground, and Joan gave a single cry of pain and terror as her banner wobbled for a second and then, its owner torn away from it, fell to the ground.

Pasquerel was beside her almost before he could think. The arrow had pierced her shoulder so deeply that the head of it was protruding from her back, its ugly metal gleaming with wet blood when Pasquerel gently rolled her onto her side. Suddenly, the bright and shining maiden, the leader of an army, the inspiration of the masses, was just a seventeen-year-old girl lying in the dirt and crying as she bled. She was dreadfully, frighteningly human, clinging to Pasquerel's hand, scared and wounded.

Her soldiers were just as shaken, but they rushed to her aid. Carrying her away from the heat of battle, they attempted to do what they could for her. Despite her pain and fear, when a soldier arrived and offered to heal her with witchcraft, Joan immediately refused, stating that she would rather die than sin. Instead, the local healers did what they could. It wasn't much. In the modern era, she would have gone into surgery, been given strong painkillers, and been cleaned and made comfortable. But this was the fifteenth century. Healers had not yet learned to wash their hands. They treated her with cotton, oil, and bacon fat. There was no anesthetic or analgesic as they dragged the arrow from her shoulder.

* * * *

When Joan was carried broken from the battlefield, the hearts of the French soldiers all seemed to go with her, torn and bloodied just as she was. They continued to fight as the day grew longer and longer, but with every hour, they seemed to tire faster. The English, jeering that they had killed the witch, rallied and held their fortress with more confidence. By late afternoon, Dunois had to face the fact that his men were faltering. Promising as their first assault had been, he couldn't deny that they were nothing without Joan.

With a heavy heart, Dunois decided to call off his men and try again the next day. When Joan heard the news, she dragged herself from the place where she was lying. Weak and pale but resolute, she begged Dunois to wait just a few minutes before giving the order. He didn't have the heart to deny her this request. She called for her horse, pulled herself into the saddle, and rode away to a nearby vineyard.

Among these grapevines, Joan sat and prayed. Her white stallion stood over her as if on guard; the gentle spring breeze stirred the deep green of the leaves around her, and the sounds of battle were muffled and distant. She breathed the peace deeply, bowed her head, and focused her every thought on the God she trusted. And she heard the voices.

* * * *

The soldiers couldn't understand why Dunois hadn't called them off yet. What hope did they have? La Pucelle, the Maid who was leading them, had been wounded. Some believed that she must have been killed or she would have been back by now. Had she abandoned them? Had God abandoned them? Every doubt gnawed deeper and deeper into their mental strength, even as every blow, every mine they dug, and every cannon they launched ate away at their physical power. They had been fighting for hours. Dusk was creeping into the western sky, and yet Les Tourelles held, the English somehow seeming invincible. The French didn't want to fight anymore. They just wanted to give up and go home.

Then, they heard it. The pure and piercing voice, rising above the brutal grunts and thuds of the battle.

"*Tout est vostre—et y entrez*!" it cried. "All is yours, go in!"

It was Joan. She came rushing up to them, carrying a scaling ladder despite her wounded arm, and her eyes were lit with hope. Her presence among them ignited them, the glimmer of her shapely armor the spark that they needed to rise into a blazing flame. She flung herself at the walls, her banner held high, shouting for them to join her. The English, who had believed she was dead, faltered. Had this witch risen from the grave, or had she miraculously been raised from the dead? Either way, it was a daunting prospect. They hesitated for just long enough. The French surged into the bastille, forcing the English back. Back to the drawbridge. Back to the last barbican of Les Tourelles. Back from the entire southern bank of the Loire, until every last Englishman had been forced from the Les Tourelles complex, from Orléans itself.

That night, Les Tourelles was retaken by the French. The next morning, the English surrendered. The sign that the examiners at Poitiers had asked for had been provided: somehow, this peasant girl who seemed to be aided by divine grace had arrived in a city on the verge of surrender and in little more than a week brought an impossible victory.

It was official. Joan of Arc was the Maid of Orléans, the heroine that France had been waiting for.

Chapter 11 – The Battle of Patay

French morale had never been higher. It was June 18th, 1429, about six weeks after the wonderful victory at Orléans, and the French had been campaigning throughout the Loire Valley ever since the siege had been lifted. And for the first time in decades, they were winning.

After weeks of attacking English-controlled fortifications, the French had put the English army to flight. Now, spurred onward and commanded by Joan of Arc, the French were pursuing their enemies up an old Roman road toward the town of Patay. Scouts had been sent to search for the English but had not yet returned with word of their whereabouts. In the meantime, the vanguard continued on the road, riding past stands of thick forest and brush. Despite the fact that they knew they were riding through enemy territory and that the surrounding vegetation was so thick that an opposing army could well be concealed nearby, the French moved with confidence. The Maid of Orléans had told them that they would have another victory today, and they believed her. The commanders had asked her where they would find the English, hoping that her saints would have told her. Her answer was cryptic but inspired courage: "Ride boldly on, we will have good guidance."

So now the vanguard of eighty knights, led by La Hire—who had also fought alongside Joan at Orléans—was riding briskly and without fear. Patay was in sight; the English had been fleeing all day, but the French horses were fresh, and their riders spurred them on with a new confidence. Joan, leading the main body of the French army, was right behind them. They believed they had nothing to fear.

They were only a few miles from Patay when the guidance that Joan had prophesied apparently came to their aid. Riding through the countryside, the clatter of the horses' feet and the clang of armor had been spooking small wild creatures all morning. There was a sudden rustle from the woods, then the sound of hooves on the road. Some of the horses were startled, and the knights scrambled to maintain control over them, looking around wildly to see what had just come crashing out of the woods.

It was a stag. Majestic, graceful, it launched itself over the road in flight, its dark eyes wide, its white tail thrown up as it fled. Its legs were thin as shadows but carried it across the ground with breathtaking speed, its spreading antlers thrown back over its shoulders. The knights and horses settled, feeling foolish for being startled by a deer. The stag fled, disappearing into the woods. Then they heard the shouting. Pausing, the knights listened as male voices filled the peaceful countryside, a clamor that could only come from a large group of men. And they were shouting in English. The stag, in its panic, had run directly into the English army, giving away their position.

La Hire quickly discovered that the English were still scrambling to put together their usual defenses—a line of sharpened stakes in front of lines of longbowmen, a formation that had been all but impenetrable to cavalry during the entire war—and called for his cavalry. While messengers raced back to the army to tell them that the English had been found, La Hire called up his men, set them against the English, and charged.

* * * *

Ever since Orléans, the French army had been enjoying victory after victory, and with each fight that they won, the Dauphin was placing more and more trust in the leadership of Joan. When she met with him the day after the English retreated from Orléans, he was a changed man—exuberant with joy and so ecstatic that some chroniclers describe him as having almost kissed her when he saw her, so overwhelmed was he with relief and happiness. Joan had done what no one had thought could be done. She had lifted the siege or, according to her, had been the instrument that God Himself used to lift the siege.

Now the English had been put to flight, and Charles had several options when it came to what to do next. The most sensible thing would be to push for a campaign toward Paris or Normandy, thereby incrementally increasing the territories that he controlled.

But Joan had other ideas. Attending the councils of war when she could, she insisted that their focus needed to be on the next part of the mission that the voices had given her: crowning Charles officially as the king of France. This could only be done in Reims, the city where generations upon generations of kings had held their coronation ceremonies. The difficulty was that Reims was miles and miles into enemy territory, much farther than Paris, and of little strategic significance. Yet Joan was adamant. Her voices had told her to go, and she was determined that she was going.

Having seen what had just come to pass at Orléans, Charles found that he couldn't say no to her. She had to be the saint, the hero, the savior that France had been waiting for. He gave her permission to lead an offensive campaign through the Loire Valley, heading for Reims. Through the beginning of June, Joan rode alongside the Duke of Alençon, who was one of her most fervent supporters especially after she saved his life during a battle at

Jargeau by warning him about a cannon that was about to fire at him. The duke jumped out of the way, and another man standing nearby was killed. It awoke a sense of loyalty in Alençon, and he did everything that Joan advised him to do.

It may have seemed a senseless strategy to listen to this uneducated girl, who usually advocated for direct attacks even when faced with unlikely odds, but it worked. In the five days between June 12th and June 17th, the French beat the English army out of the Loire Valley despite reinforcements that had arrived from Paris. First Jargeau, then Meung, and then Beaugency fell before them. Now the English were running north, and the French were hot on their heels, ready for another great victory.

* * * *

La Hire's cavalry charge surged toward the hedgerows where the English archers were concealed. Panicking, the English line started to crumble before the cavalry could even reach it. A scattered volley of arrows sprang forth, bouncing off plate armor, but while one or two knights screamed and fell, the charge continued. Faced with a wall of armored horses barreling toward them, the archers turned tail and fled.

It was not so much a battle as it was a massacre. The English put up almost no resistance. They were cut down as they ran, the panicking army utterly routed, scattering into the countryside. By the time Joan and the main army reached the battlefield, the fighting was mostly over, the entire field strewn with the torn and broken corpses of thousands of Englishmen.

The sight broke Joan's heart even though the English were her enemies. Dismounting from her horse, she knelt down beside the nearest dying English soldier, cradled his head in her hands, and tried her best to soothe him as he faded slowly into death.

Two thousand Englishmen died that day; of the French, only about a hundred fell. It was the humiliating Battle of Agincourt all over again, except this time in reverse. The French had won, and they were determined to keep on winning.

Chapter 12 – Beans for the Apocalypse

The army that set out from Orléans in late June was completely different than the one Joan had first led out of Chinon. Then, she had just a handful of men, all of them dispirited and barely clinging onto the hope that her white banner had given them. Now, her men numbered as many as twelve thousand. These were knights and common soldiers and even ordinary citizens of the surrounding towns who had armed themselves with swords and spears and mounted their little farm ponies to join the cause. Everyone wanted to follow Joan, wherever she led.

And despite some misgivings from other commanders who believed that the army should turn to Normandy instead, she was leading them to Reims. Charles met the army at Gien the evening after they left Orléans; he was wildly excited, radiant at the prospect of finally being given the crown that he'd been born for. Joan was serene as ever, believing and insisting firmly that they were going to get to Reims and that Charles was going to be crowned, no matter what dared to stand in their way.

As it turned out, not much did stand in their way. The English believed that Joan was a witch, a terrifying sorceress whose curses were invincible; she struck terror into their hearts, and their resistance melted before her, morale plummeting as their commanders desperately tried to keep control over their panicking men. The towns may have been occupied by Englishmen, but they were populated by the French who were willing to ally themselves once again to the Dauphin now that word had it that he was traveling with a bona fide saint. As they moved nearer to Reims, the French army hardly had cause to strike a single blow. City after city flung open their gates and surrendered, welcoming Charles as their king. It was less of a campaign and more of a victory march on the road to Reims.

It was during this time, however, that Joan—for the first and possibly last time—performed an act of violence. On June 29th, as the army headed out of Gien to start its march, Joan noticed a group of young women hanging around the gates of the city. In an age where thousands of men were torn away from their wives and families and spent weeks or months on the road, unaccompanied and often bored, prostitution flourished. Wherever the army went, prostitutes went with it, always on the edges of the camp, and this day was no exception. As the army left Gien, Joan saw that some of the young men had noticed the prostitutes. They headed toward them, utterly distracted from their mission, and Joan flew into a rage. Charging toward them on her horse, she ripped out her sword. Terrified by the wrath of their leader, the men scrambled away, the prostitutes fleeing, but they were too slow for Joan. Ignoring the prostitutes, she set furiously upon the men, slapping them with the flat of her sword. They were safe from any cuts by the edge, but the flat was hard enough, and Joan swung it with a strength born of fury. She was only about five feet tall, yet she struck the nearest soldier hard enough that the sword broke.

The soldiers thus chastised, Joan returned to the head of the army, sweaty and wild-eyed with anger. No man even dared to look at a prostitute as they headed off on their march. One of their first stops, the town of Auxerre, was familiar to Joan; she had visited it on her journey from Vaucouleurs to Chinon, sneaking inside the city walls in order to hear Mass. Now, she rode boldly toward it at the head of a victorious army. While Auxerre remained loyal to its fealty of the Duke of Burgundy, it did not resist the French, instead supplying the army with provisions; after a brief rest, they continued toward a city that must have held considerable heartache for Charles: Troyes.

* * * *

It was in Troyes that Charles's own mother had signed off his birthright, giving away the country to an English king. Bitterness must have filled Charles's heart as they neared the city. If only Isabeau had not signed that treaty, Charles would have been king by now—a king at war, certainly, but at least a true and official king. He would not have had to fight tooth and nail across his own country just to be able to wear the crown that he believed he'd been born for.

Yet here he was, approaching Troyes itself with a vast force of loyal soldiers, led by this strange and yet undeniably charismatic young woman. Joan rode beside the king, now on a black charger; the white banner flapped above her head which bore a short and boyish haircut, still growing out after she had been disguised as a man for the journey to Chinon. It was early morning when Troyes came into view, and it was immediately obvious that this was the first city that would not be going down without a fight. Even though the garrison at Troyes numbered only 500 men, they sallied out courageously against Charles's huge force. After a brief but intense fight, they were driven back into Troyes. Little or no damage was done to the French army, but the facts were clear: Troyes was going to resist.

The city that had disinherited Charles would now continue to be a thorn in his side. Confident that it wouldn't be long before Troyes submitted, Charles ordered his men to dig in and prepare for a siege. The Anglo-Burgundian garrison was vastly outnumbered, and Charles was sure it wouldn't be long before they gave up.

There was just one problem: The French army had nothing to eat. The supplies they had bought at Auxerre were long gone; now, they found themselves camping in the countryside, deep into enemy territory, with thousands of human and equine mouths to feed. Summertime allowed for the horses to graze, but the army was made up of finicky French knights who were used to luxurious cuisine.

The solution to this issue was, like Joan of Arc herself, about as strange and unorthodox as they came. The previous winter, a wandering friar had made his way into Troyes. His message was that the end of the world was at hand, that Jesus was coming back that summer, and that the people of Troyes needed to be ready to feed an angelic host. For that reason, instead of planting the usual wheat crop, the farmers of Troyes and its surroundings had planted all of their fields with an early crop of beans.

No angelic army descended upon Troyes as Brother Richard had promised. But there was an army, and it was hungry, and it arrived just as the beans began to ripen.

* * * *

Troyes continued to hold out stubbornly for several days as the French army surrounded the city. Charles began to wonder if besieging the city was really worth his while; their aim was to reach Reims, not to capture everything in their path. He started to discuss his options with his commanders, most of whom were in favor of retreating and going back to Gien instead. One of the older men finally succeeded in persuading them to consult with Joan before making any decisions, considering that they had followed Joan this far.

Her response was predictable. She believed that Troyes was going to fall soon, within the next couple of days, and Charles just had to stand his ground. Just as she had asked Robert de Baudricourt to tell Charles that he had to stand firm against his enemies, long before the name of Jeanne d'Arc meant anything to anyone in France, now she was continuing to exhort the Dauphin to be brave and persevere.

Gathering the army, Joan ordered the soldiers to start building outworks in the moat of Troyes, preparing for a full-scale offensive. Her white banner had given them victory before; they trusted that it would do so again, and they worked fervently and fearlessly.

The Anglo-Burgundians inside Troyes had already heard all the stories about the witch of Orléans and her terrifying powers. They watched in dismay as Joan's outworks took shape and saw, with horror, that she had arrayed them in as skillful a manner as would any experienced military commander. Her apparent supernatural powers frightened them, and they hurriedly sent forth some of the city's leaders to attempt peaceful negotiations with the French army.

Among these was that same Brother Richard whose preaching had furnished the Frenchmen with their beans. Although he was suspicious of Joan at first, fearfully sprinkling holy water at her to ward off her demons, he would later become one of her allies. Nonetheless, despite the friar's misgivings, an agreement was reached allowing the garrison to escape and surrender the city. Later that morning, the gates of Troyes were thrown wide open. And the Dauphin Charles, overjoyed and triumphant, could enter at last the city where his own family had betrayed him.

Chapter 13 – The French King Crowned

Joan of Arc at the Coronation of King Charles VII by Jean Auguste Dominique Ingres, 1854. The clergyman depicted is Jean Pasquerel, Joan's companion.
https://commons.wikimedia.org/wiki/File:Ingres_coronation_charles_vii.jpg

Reims Cathedral, July 17th, 1429. It was here that the first king of France—then king of the Franks—had been baptized by Saint Remi almost a thousand years ago. And ever since then, for generation upon generation, every king of France had been crowned here in a ceremony as ancient as it was holy and as venerated as it was elaborate. The vaulted ceilings rose up into the sky, the walls gilded and lavishly decorated in a show of shameless splendor, and below the towering height of the roof stood some of the highest-ranking people in all of France, most notably, the young king who knelt by the altar, ready to receive his crown at last.

And among them all was Joan of Arc, a peasant girl from the borders of Lorraine. A nobody, and yet her name was on the lips of every man in France and England alike. She could neither read nor write, she had no schooling, and she was one of the most low-born people in the entire country. And yet here she stood, not only an onlooker at the coronation of the king of France but an instrumental part of the events that had led up to this very moment. She had shed her fair share of blood, sweat, and tears to bring Charles to Reims, and now she watched in glowing satisfaction and joy as the ceremony took place.

The coronation ceremony was an elaborate one. One of its key components was a vial of holy oil, said to have been brought to Saint Remi for the baptism of Clovis I by a dove descended from heaven. The oil was housed in a pure golden reliquary, which contained a crystal vial, and it was used sparingly and reverently upon Charles's back and shoulders just as it had been used on all of his ancestors that had been king. Then, the constable of France entered, bearing a royal and elaborately carved sword that was used symbolically to knight the king. This particular sword, often since known as the Sword of the Maid in honor of Joan, has since been lost to time; it vanished somewhere during the French Revolution many years later. The king was then awarded his golden spurs, a sword, his royal robes, ring and scepter, and finally, the crown of France. At last, the bejeweled crown was lowered onto the head of the Dauphin Charles. He was Dauphin no longer. He was the king.

Throughout the ceremony—which lasted about five hours—Joan had been standing motionless near the king, watching in contented silence and holding her banner. It was a tattered thing by now, worn throughout the many battles, but the hope it held still beat hard in the hearts of every Frenchman as they finally beheld their king upon the throne. Joan herself didn't move until the king was finally crowned. Then her restraint seemed to have left her. She threw aside her banner and flung herself at Charles's feet, just as she had done months ago when she identified the king among three hundred courtiers. "Noble king!" she cried out, addressing him as "king" for the first time since that first meeting. "Now is accomplished the will of God, who wished me to lift the siege of Orléans." She was crying openly, tears streaming down her cheeks as she clung to Charles's legs. With the emotion running as high as it was inside the cathedral, it was the last straw. The bystanders broke down into tears as Joan clung to the feet of her king and rejoiced. She had done what her voices had told her to do. She had brought the king to Reims.

With that, the ceremony was closed by a fanfare of trumpets. The trumpet players were so filled with emotion that their fanfare seemed to rock the very cathedral; in the words of one of the witnesses, "it seemed the vaults of the church must be riven apart."

* * * *

Reims had capitulated to the approaching French army, throwing open its gates without any resistance and welcoming the Dauphin inside for his coronation. Now that he was crowned King Charles VII, the king knew that his work was far from done. France was still in a state of civil war, and the English were everywhere, especially swarming over his capital—Paris.

Joan wasn't done with the war, either. Despite the fact that the battles seemed to have had a profound emotional effect on her, she was ready for more. Soon after the coronation, she informed the king that her voices had instructed her to take the army and head directly to Paris for an assault that aimed to retake the city. The Duke of Alençon predictably supported her in this decision, but Charles was not so easily persuaded. Even after the victories that Joan had brought them, part of him seemed to remain a little suspicious. He refused to follow her blindly and instead called a council to discuss what to do next, where it was decided that it would be a wiser move to attempt to negotiate a truce with the Duke of Burgundy, still a key ally for the English.

In the meantime, Joan stayed in Reims, having little to do but still being of importance to the people. After four months of constant activity, it must have been a relief to have some respite and stay in one city for more than a few weeks. And it must have been a strange new world for this peasant girl who had never been in contact with the higher classes outside of the military. She was one of the most famous—and also the most powerful, considering that most of the French soldiers would have followed her anywhere, even if it was against their commanders' orders—people in France, and yet none of it seemed to affect her behavior. She refused to indulge in the luxuries that were available to her in Reims, often refusing even to eat meat or vegetables. Instead, Joan often opted to have only a little bread, perhaps longing for the simple diet that she had once had when she was just an ordinary young girl in Domrémy. She often said since the beginning of her rise that if it was up to her, she would have stayed behind in the village. She had a far greater desire to tend sheep and spin wool than to lead armies and crown kings. Yet her voices compelled her; she insisted that the saints were telling her what to do, and Joan lived to obey their orders.

Yet this time, Charles would not be convinced to march directly on Paris. Instead, he was negotiating with Philip of Burgundy, ignoring Joan and her voices. It would turn out to be a terrible mistake.

Chapter 14 – The Siege of Paris

Joan at the Siege of Paris
https://commons.wikimedia.org/wiki/File:Le_si%C3%A8ge_de_Paris_en_1429_par_Jeanne_d%27Arc_-_Martial.jpg

While Joan continued to urge the newly-crowned King Charles VII to attack Paris without delay, the king dug in his toes. He refused to move on Paris until he had finished his negotiations with the Duke of Burgundy, no matter how earnest Joan pleaded with him to heed her words. It would have been easy after all that Joan had achieved during her time with the army to feel betrayed and affronted by Charles's lack of trust in her, but if she did, she didn't show it. Instead, she accompanied her friend the Duke of Alençon on an almost aimless march, capturing towns surrounding Reims. Most of these surrendered without any resistance.

Meanwhile, as Charles attempted to reach some kind of pact with Philip, the deceitful Duke of Burgundy was only participating in negotiations because he was playing for time. Even as he smiled and nodded in his meetings with the French, even as he played friendly on the surface, Philip was busy giving orders to his men to have Paris fortified against a potential attack from the French. He only ceased negotiations when his fortifications were finished. The entire exercise had been utterly fruitless; instead of coming close to peace, Charles had succeeded only in giving his enemy the upper hand. He would have done well to heed Joan's words. Yet he didn't. And for that, the French army would pay the price.

* * * *

It was late August before the negotiations finally came to an end, and Charles decided that an attack on Paris would be necessary after all. Joan and the rest of the army had been moving across the country toward the capital, and on August 26th, 1429, she and her men captured a small village near Paris and established themselves and their troops at La Chapelle. Here, they started sending small groups to the city to reconnoiter the gates and determine just how much Philip had been able to improve the defenses.

What they saw brought them great dismay. Paris had been founded centuries ago, at the end of the third century BCE, and over the passage of more than a millennium, it had only grown in importance and strength. The fortress was already almost impregnable before the Duke of Burgundy started to fortify it against the attack that Joan now found herself leading. Now, it was an intimidating sight, even though Joan and other commanders knew its garrison only held about 3,000 men. Charles's army numbered 10,000, but they did not have the advantage of the strong defenses that stood guard all around the heart of the city.

Joan headed off to a small chapel at La Chapelle, known as St. Genevieve's Chapel, a few days after their arrival in the area. Her purpose was to pray, and it is easy to see why she chose to seek her divine inspiration from Saint Genevieve. Born more than a thousand years before, she had also been a virgin saint, a woman who had traveled all over the country preaching and healing. St. Genevieve, too, had claimed to have seen visions of saints and angels, perhaps even in a similar way to how Joan had seen them. She must have felt like the only person in the world with whom Joan could identify with, as Joan's voices continued to speak to her, urging her to get to Paris and to take France back for its rightful and recently anointed king. Joan knelt down there in the peace of the little chapel, and she prayed, hoping that her voices would return to guide her.

That same chapel still stands today, although Paris's streets have grown and swollen so much that it is now a part of Paris itself. The very spot where Joan knelt in prayer can still be visited today. As the sun set, Joan took her place, and as the night wore on, she didn't move, staying there, her entire mind focused on listening for her voices. It was dawn, and her body was cold, stiff, and aching when she arose from her knees, but Joan was filled with determination. They were going to take Paris, and she was going to lead her army forward to victory once again.

Charles only reached Paris on September 7th, having been wasting his time once again in an agony of indecision. As soon as he arrived with some reinforcements, Joan and the Duke of Alençon gave the order to attack. Joan herself rode at the head of the army. The Anglo-Burgundians watched in trepidation as she came into view, a feminine figure clad in gleaming steel, astride a black stallion that flashed in the noonday sun. A breeze unfurled her banner above her head; pure white against a landscape ablaze with the warm colors of autumn, it was a symbol of hope for the French, and a thing of terror for all who stood against them.

This time there would be no attempts to hold Joan back. The commanders knew that their men fought best if the Maid of Orléans was at their head.

And at the lead Joan was. Seizing her banner, she called up the men. They burst forward, rushing toward the walls of Paris with unrelenting zeal. Joan was at the very front of the army, her banner leading the way as they charged the moat. The air was filled with the crack and thunder of the culverins—medieval cannons—mounted on the nearby buttes; for every volley that France fired, the Parisians returned, raining stone missiles down onto Joan's men. Crossbows twanged, their heavy bolts pouring into the ranks; swords clashed as they threw grappling hooks up the walls and started climbing, fighting hard to prevent being cut down. It was a chaos of death and destruction, but according to one eyewitness named Perceval de Cagny, not a single one of Joan's men was severely wounded, even though many were struck down by cannonballs.

Yet the Parisians did not back down, and the fortifications of the great city held firm. Hour after hour, Joan's men strove against the defenses, and many times they came perilously close to overrunning them entirely, but each time the Parisians managed to push them back. The sun slipped low in the sky, bathing the fighters first in gold, then in twilight as dusk settled over the landscape. Throughout it all, Joan did not waver. She stood upon the outworks, her banner held high, and called them forward with the voice they had followed so many times to victory.

With her white banner flying so proudly, she made a perfect target. A Parisian crossbowman took careful aim at her, hefting the heavy crossbow upon his shoulder. Then he took fire. The bolt sang through the air, an ugly, heavy thing, deadly and brutal in its simplicity. There was a butcher's noise, a slicing of flesh, and Joan collapsed. The bolt had pierced her thigh. She crumpled to the earth, blood bursting out from the jagged wound in her leg from the crossbow bolt jutting cruelly from her young flesh. Crying out in pain, she still somehow managed to struggle into a sitting position. She saw that her soldiers had faltered, and even as she clutched her wound and felt her own warm blood sliding between her fingers, she knew she had to call back the hope that was in them. Raising her voice, she continued to urge them forward, and they renewed the assault.

It wasn't long, however, before Charles decided that the fighting was fruitless. The men had been striving against Paris's defenses for hours, and they were exhausted. He ordered a retreat. Joan had to be bodily carried from the battlefield as she cried that her voices had told her to continue the assault.

The next day, Joan, lying in her bed at La Chapelle with her leg bound up, told Charles that if he attacked Paris again today, the city would be his. But Charles had found her a lot easier to believe in when she was an armored maiden on a horse, not this pale and injured girl lying in a sickbed. He called off the attack. The Siege of Paris was declared a failure, and it became the first defeat that the French would suffer since Joan of Arc joined their ranks.

Chapter 15 – Peace

The defeat at Paris seemed to leach all of the fire and energy back out of King Charles once more. Even though victory seemed to be so close, he had to face one undeniable fact: he couldn't afford to pay his troops. The towns they had captured had only just started to pay taxes once again; the huge army that Charles had amassed in order to get to Reims now needed to be paid, and his coffers were empty after years of collecting taxes from almost only Bourges. Instead, Charles had to disband most of the army, sending many of his soldiers back home.

Winter was fast approaching. As Joan recuperated from the wound she had received at Paris, the leaves fell from the trees, and the first frost started to nip at the landscape at night. So, too, did the bloom of Joan's power begin to fade. Even though her voices reportedly never left her, Charles's confidence did. He was no longer the desperate "King of Bourges" that Joan had met in Chinon more than six months ago. No, he was king now, a king who had received the holy anointing and conquered more territory in three months than France had been able to reclaim in years of war. Suddenly, Joan was no longer needed.

It can't be said that Charles mistreated her during this time. He seemed almost anxious for her to be happy, supplying her with luxury upon luxury, an opulent existence that would have been almost incomprehensible for this ordinary farm girl who had grown up among peasants. Joan's family had been considered wealthy because they always had something on the table for dinner; many of the people that she grew up with had gone to bed hungry, so those who were considered to be well-off simply had their needs supplied. There was room for joy and fun, but there was absolutely none for excess or luxury in their simple lives. Yet now Joan found herself residing in a vast mansion, waited on hand and foot by ladies who were much higher-born than herself. She was given flamboyant clothes to wear and offered the best delicacies that Charles could find to eat. A golden mantle was made for her to be worn over her battle-stained armor. But none of this was what Joan wanted. Her heart yearned for just one thing—to honor the voices. And they told her to go out and defeat the enemy that still controlled the majority of France.

For Charles and his advisers, however, the decision was final. They had believed in Joan when they had no other option, but now that they felt fairly secure in their position, they would no longer place any faith in her. Never again would Jeanne d'Arc ride at the very head of the army. Instead, she could lead small bands on occasional skirmishes, usually only against the bandits and freebooters that plagued France now that an entire army had suddenly found itself with nothing to do. While Charles negotiated truces with the Dukes of Burgundy and Bedford, Joan felt cooped up, trapped, and cornered without any way to obey the saints that she believed were guiding her. One historian chose to use the words "mortal languishment" to describe her condition, and they were likely accurate.

Some of her allies, however, did make an effort to help her. The Duke of Alençon attempted to arrange a campaign into Normandy, but Charles absolutely refused to allow Joan to accompany him. Disheartened, the duke disbanded his troops. It was, eventually, Charles himself that would allow Joan back onto the battlefield once more. Regardless of how much pain and worry he had put Joan through by keeping her with his court, it appears that Charles did care for her welfare, and he finally had to face the fact that keeping Joan off the battlefield may be protecting her body, but it was breaking her heart. He allowed her to join a small campaign that was touring France and subduing the little towns that were left within Charles's territory that had not yet surrendered.

One of these was the town of St. Pierre-le-Moutier. It was a small town, but when Joan reached it with a long-time friend and military commander named Jean d'Aulon commanding her troops, it immediately put up a strenuous resistance. Joan's little army attacked, urged on by the Maiden who was adamant that the city was going to fall. Yet it appeared that this battle would be a hideous echo of what had happened at Paris. The assault was a disaster. D'Aulon sounded the retreat, pulling his troops back to safety; he himself was wounded, and so were many of his men. He was struggling to retreat on an injured leg when he noticed, to his horror, that Joan had not heeded the order. Instead, she stood against the bombardment of the defenders almost alone, only half a dozen courageous men holding their ground beside her.

D'Aulon had been personally charged by the king not to allow anything to happen to Joan, so he couldn't leave her behind. Hurrying toward her, he shouted out, thinking that perhaps she hadn't heard the order. "Jeanne, withdraw, withdraw!" he bellowed as his army stampeded into the distance in wild panic. "You are alone!"

Joan's face was radiant as she turned toward him, as if bathed in heavenly light. That otherworldly glow was in her blue eyes again as she spoke. "I still have with me fifty thousand men!" she called, her laughter filled with confidence. "To work, to work!" Her raised voice rang across the countryside. Its clear tone seemed to wake the retreating army from its fervent panic, and as d'Aulon worked together with Joan to rally the men, they pulled themselves together and renewed the attack. When St. Pierre-le-Moutier finally fell after the second attack, it must have felt like redemption to Joan after the failure at Paris. It did lead many of her contemporaries—and historians—to question whether Paris might have fallen if Joan had those extra few hours she asked for.

Either way, St. Pierre-le-Moutier was to be Joan's last great victory. Peace was starting to descend upon France, a time of relative ease and respite for the people. But for Joan, her glory days had ended. Her suffering was just beginning.

Chapter 16 – Capture

The treaty that Charles had succeeded in negotiating with the Burgundians was short-lived. By the spring of 1430, the fragile peace had disintegrated, and Burgundian soldiers began to march upon French towns once more. The Duke of Burgundy's plan was to seize the towns and cities along the Oise River, thereby protecting Paris from another attempt by the French army—he knew that the city had come perilously close to falling.

One of these towns, and one of the first that he planned to besiege, was Compiègne. It was a small town and not thoroughly fortified, but its inhabitants had declared their loyalty to King Charles VII shortly after his coronation; now, the Duke of Burgundy was determined to reclaim it. He issued a letter to the town's garrison, giving them a harsh reminder that, legally, the city belonged to him. It was not an empty threat, but it was a threat that did not intimidate the citizens of Compiègne. Instead of submitting to the Duke of Burgundy, they prepared for war.

Joan knew as early as March 1430 that danger awaited Compiègne; whether she had been told about it by her voices or learned about it by more earthly means remains unclear. Either way, she knew that she had to do something. Charles refused to give her any troops to command; it was a sad thing for a woman who had once led the entire army, but it seemed that Charles was content with the victories they had won and had no desire to gamble any more of his power on Joan and her visions. But she was far from powerless. She remained one of the most famous women of the era, and the Frenchmen would rally around her, king or no king. By April, she had put together several hundred men and led them to Compiègne in early May—probably without the king's knowledge.

For three weeks, Joan resided in the city, relishing her newfound freedom. Even though she had always honored Charles as her king, even when he was not king yet, her obedience to her voices was more important to her than anything else. At any rate, Charles had not tried to stop her. Perhaps he believed that she was comparatively safe in Compiègne, although he did send some reinforcements there, so it was evident that he knew Burgundy would attack the city.

The Burgundian troops had already been encamped around the city when Joan and her troops got there. They had slipped past under cover of darkness, and as the weeks passed, the Burgundians continued to tighten the noose. All the while, Joan and the commander of the city—Guillaume de Flavy—were working together on a plan to free Compiègne. It involved a sortie against the Burgundian camps with the plan to retreat back into Compiègne if needed, but the goal was to put the Burgundians to flight so that a retreat would not be necessary.

The plan was put into action on May 24th. Joan led the army out in the late afternoon, a dazzling and resplendent figure all aglitter in her golden doublet, the edges of it flowing over the haunches of her stallion as her cavalry galloped after her toward the first of the camps. But there was trouble brewing. An English force had arrived to assist Burgundy, and it was heading rapidly toward the city, toward Joan and her little army.

Back at the raised road that led back into Compiègne, Guillaume de Flavy and his men were charged with protecting the road to ensure that the cavalry could safely retreat if it was needed. They watched with trepidation as Joan led her charge. Thundering into the ranks of the Burgundians, led by that white banner, the French slammed into their enemies; from the boulevard near the city walls, cannons cried out, their loud crack filling the sweet spring air, and the arriving English were thrown back by heavy fire.

But so was Joan. Her cavalry was pushed back and forced to retreat a short distance to regroup. Several of her men glanced back to the inviting open road back to the city, guarded by a lowered drawbridge and a raised portcullis. But Joan soon put any thoughts of retreat out of their minds. Calling out that victory was sure, she brandished her banner and set spurs to her horse. They renewed their charge, crashed into the Burgundians, and this time, they were victorious.

However, as the first line of Burgundians cracked, another camp was galloping to their aid. Joan swung her cavalry around just in time to face them. She and her men found themselves hard-pressed on both sides, struggling viciously against their attackers; Joan was always in the thick of it, never striking a blow but always holding up her banner and shouting out encouragements to any who could hear her.

Yet this time, it wasn't enough. The English reinforcements were starting to break through. Wave after wave of enemies rushed down upon Joan's soldiers, and their courage began to fail them faced with such an overwhelming number of enemies. They were vastly outnumbered, and Joan saw it. She stayed calm, rallying her men with shouts of encouragement, knowing that her plan had allowed for a retreat if necessary. She ordered the retreat, and her men swung their horses about and kicked them on toward home. The horses didn't need to be told twice. They rushed back toward

Compiègne, all except for Joan's stallion. Held back, he fought and plunged, wanting to follow his allies, yet Joan held him in, her banner snapping above her head, her only protection. She only let him go once every last one of her surviving men had torn themselves away from the battle. Then she followed at the very rear of her troops, keeping herself between them and the enemy, just as she had always been at the forefront of every charge.

They galloped toward Compiègne, their horses' hooves ringing on the raised road. It was so close. Safety was only a tantalizing few yards away, with the first of Joan's men already reaching the drawbridge. She herself was on the road, crossing the bridge, when Guillaume de Flavy screamed out an order to close the drawbridge. The Burgundians were hot on the heels of the French, and he believed that closing the city was the only way to save it. Or perhaps his treachery was intentional; the real story behind his actions has been lost to time. Yet either way, we know one thing. The drawbridge slammed shut. The portcullis fell to the earth. And Joan of Arc, the heroine of France, was trapped. Behind her, she had a horde of furious enemies determined to take down this witch, and in front, a door shut to her by her own friends.

A handful of Joan's own personal guard had stayed near her, and now they turned to face the mass of Burgundians bearing down upon them. It was a fight that they knew they would lose, even as they knew they had no choice but to fight it. One by one, they were sliced down, butchered by their enemies, until only Joan was left. She wheeled her horse around, trying to find a way to safety, yet there was none. It was a rough Burgundian archer who reached her first, a leering man, his face twisted with hatred at the sight of this woman who had done what nobody else had been able to do. Before Joan could get away, he seized her glittering golden doublet and yanked. She was ripped from the saddle and slammed into the earth, her armor dented and stained with dust, the breath knocked from her where she fell.

* * * *

Joan had little choice other than to surrender. She was immediately captured and dragged from the battlefield by her enemies. While Compiègne had been defended and was safe from Burgundy for the time being, the battle could hardly be considered a victory. The greatest weapon France had had throughout the Hundred Years' War, one of the most unique, most unlikely, and yet most successful military commanders it had ever known had been lost. She was gone, carried off into captivity, lost to France. And it would not be long before she was lost to this world, too.

Chapter 17 – Captive

Joan was carried off to the nearby castle of Beaurevoir where she was to begin her long captivity. It was not an unexpected thing for her. As early as the beginning of April, she testified that St. Catherine and St. Margaret had visited her and told her that she would soon be captured and forced to endure a long and unhappy imprisonment. Joan begged them to make it otherwise, to allow her to be killed in battle rather than face being trapped in some enemy fortress, but the voices were unrelenting. God would help her, they said, but there was no other way. She was going to become a prisoner.

And now, a prisoner she was—perhaps the most valuable prisoner in the history of the Hundred Years' War, even though kings and princes had found themselves behind bars at some point during its sad and difficult course. Valuable as she was, however, she was not treated well. Decades ago, King John II of France had been imprisoned in England; he had been given a luxurious life with court musicians and a comfortable home to call his own. None of these privileges were afforded to Joan. She had long been viewed with extreme suspicion, and now that she was in the hands of her enemies, they were not going to treat her with anything other than the harshness they felt became a sorceress.

It is a sad and bitter fact that Joan had no hope of rescue. She had effectively changed Charles from a hopeless Dauphin, on the verge of fleeing to Scotland to live a life in disgraced exile, to the King of France who commanded an army and controlled much of his country once more, yet no help would come to her from that quarter. Charles heard of her capture and all but dismissed her. He wrote a few threatening letters to England and Burgundy during Joan's captivity, yet he took no action. There was no attempt to ransom her, and Charles did not rally his army and attempt to take the castle where she was being kept. His actions smack of abandonment; his attitude, of ingratitude.

Meanwhile, Joan was stuck in the tower of Beaurevoir, constantly attended by a male guard. This immediately started to pose a problem. Much as Joan conducted herself with modesty to all accounts, she was still a woman—a young, beautiful, and shapely woman, and she started to attract unwanted attention almost at once. It is difficult to comprehend exactly how hard this treatment must have been for Joan. She had grown up in a little village that prided itself on its Catholic faith, a place made up of farmers and merchants who knew each other and had known each other for generations, a place too small for scandal. Then she had been the Maid, the virgin who was to save the kingdom, revered and always treated with respect. Now she was just a prisoner, and she found herself having to fight off the lewd advances of her guards and visitors, trying her hardest to keep herself pure the way she had vowed to her God that she would.

In her desperation, Joan turned to the same defense that she had employed on her journey to Chinon: men's clothing. The tight hosen of the era, tucked into boots, was at least some protection against those who would think to rape her. Even though her captors often tried to persuade her otherwise, she refused to wear a woman's dress. In an era when women were never seen wearing any kind of pants, it was scandalous, strange, and even—in some eyes—an act of sin. Yet to Joan, it was a panicking bid to maintain her purity.

Between her fear for her virginity and her worry over how things were faring in the rest of France, Joan was driven to extreme lengths in her attempts to escape from Beaurevoir. Her first attempt was made as early as June 6th, when she succeeded in slamming the door on her guard in the tower and tried to flee. Her plan was thwarted when a porter happened upon her at that moment and managed to recapture her.

Her next and most dangerous attempt came in October, shortly after a visit from one ribald knight who did his best to molest her.

* * * *

The very tower where Joan had tried to lock her guard away was her prison. She was allowed only one small liberty: to walk around the very top of the tower and look out over the countryside from between the battlements. It was more than sixty feet off the ground, and there was no way down: just the sheer drop of the walls down to the rocky ground below. One morning, as Joan stood in the chill autumn air, she stared down at the drop, and a thought filled her mind.

Even now, abandoned and imprisoned, Joan had no intentions of taking her own life. But a wild hope began to beat in her breast. If she, a peasant girl, could lift in only days a siege that had endured for three-quarters of a year, surely escaping from this tower was not an impossible miracle. She walked over to the battlements and stepped up onto the low wall, keeping her hands braced against the battlements on either side of her. The drop gaped below her yet failed to frighten her. Perhaps if she jumped, she could run, disappear into the countryside, and find her way back to her men.

Later, Joan would tell how her voices had arrived at that moment and begged her not to jump, urging her that it was not God's will. But this was the one time when she would choose to ignore them. Joan jumped. The wind howled against her, snagging at her growing hair, screaming in her ears as the ground rushed up closer and closer—

She struck the ground with a force that rendered her senseless. The impact should have killed her. Instead, Joan escaped with only a concussion and some scrapes and bruises; every bone in her body was still thoroughly intact.

* * * *

In November 1430, shortly after her escape attempt, Joan was sold like a piece of furniture. The Burgundians were still allied with the English, and after months of negotiations, they agreed to sell her to their English friends for the sum of 10,000 *livres tournois*. She was shipped unceremoniously to Rouen at the end of December, then an English-held fortress in France, and here her captivity began to take a turn for the worse.

While she was kept in a tower cell instead of the dungeon, Joan still had to contend with cold, darkness, damp, and pests—and these were not only in the form of rats. The English guards were even worse than the Burgundians. Joan was terrified of them, and to make matters worse, there was no walking about freely in Rouen as there had been in Beaurevoir. Perhaps because of her escape attempts, Joan was now kept not only in a cell but in chains. Her legs were shackled then chained to one another and to her bed; the chains were so tight that she could not walk without assistance. For a young woman who had never known anything but freedom, this treatment must have been utterly intolerable. She had grown up running through the fields of Domrémy then lived at the forefront of Charles's army, riding a stallion across the vastness of France; yet now it was a like a punishment to move just from her bed to the cell next door, which served as her crude and stinking toilet.

To make matters worse, the English, despite all of their laws, were determined to persecute Joan to every length they could find. Female prisoners were usually kept in a convent instead of a cell, where they were guarded by nuns and usually never shackled. Prisoners-of-war, on the other hand, were treated as roughly as Joan was. Yet at least prisoners-of-war had the faint hope of release once the war was over.

There would be none of this hope for Joan. Shortly after her arrival in Rouen, it became evident that the English had no intentions of ever setting her free. They were going to have her stand trial. And they were going to execute her, whether the trial was fair or not.

Chapter 18 – A Saint Tried for Heresy

Joan's interrogation by the Cardinal of Winchester
https://commons.wikimedia.org/wiki/File:Joan_of_arc_interrogation.jpg

Everything about Joan's trial was unfair and unjust.

For a start, there were no grounds on which to start an ecclesiastical trial. Much of her trial was recorded, and the documents concerning it have been studied extensively by all kinds of experts over the centuries, and yet none of them could find evidence that would—in the laws of that era—justify the decision to put her on trial. She was put on trial anyway, and it was obvious at once that this was no real trial. It was simply an attempt to discredit Joan as much as possible before her inevitable execution.

The court that was assembled to try Joan consisted almost entirely of Englishmen, Burgundians, and their sympathizers. Those who would dare to question the trial's agenda were secretly threatened with death if they refused to comply. To make matters worse, many of the documents involved in Joan's trial were falsified to ensure that she couldn't win. And the last blow was to refuse Joan any form of legal representation. She represented herself. She had no choice.

Yet it would soon become obvious to Joan's captors that this was not as much of a problem for her as they expected it would be. The Maid of France was about to astonish everyone around her one more time. One last time.

* * * *

February 21st, 1431. It was only a couple of months since Joan had been brought to Rouen, and already she found herself before the court, facing a roomful of enemies with not a single friend to come to her aid. She had been abandoned by everyone—everyone but her voices, and yet somehow, they seemed to be enough for her. She walked into the room utterly collected, and that was the first thing that unnerved the court. They had likely never actually seen Joan in their lives; they expected some shivering wreck, some scared and trembling wisp of a girl who had only clueless and stumbling answers. She was an illiterate peasant, after all.

Instead, walking into the room, Joan bore herself with the humility of a saint but the confidence of a queen. She gave the room a single steady glance with her strange blue eyes, and at once they could see that she was unafraid. To make matters worse, they knew—although likely she didn't—that a preliminary inquiry had already been conducted and people from her past were interviewed to establish her character. No one had been able to say anything against her, so the English knew that they were going to have their work cut out for them in order to find any kind of justification for her death.

Bishop Pierre Cauchon put the first question to Joan, a routine one concerning the oath under which she would testify. "Do you swear to speak the truth in answer to such questions as are put to you?" he asked.

Joan regarded him with a steely eye. He had expected her to meekly mumble a yes. Instead, her answer was as fearless as the one during the examination at Poitiers. "I do not know what you wish to examine me on," she said calmly, knowing full well that no one could really prove why she was on trial. "Perhaps you might ask such things that I would not tell."

This would set the tone for all of Joan's answers during the trial. She refused to accept the oath, and accordingly, she refused to give whole answers for much of the trial as well. Concerning her saints and voices, she would describe who they were and what they had said with clarity, but she refused to go into too much detail about their appearance, saying that she didn't have leave to reveal everything about them. As for her audience with Charles, she absolutely refused to share the confidential details of their first meeting. "Ask him," she told the court boldly.

But there would be no asking Charles. Charles would have none of the trial. Joan was alone before some of the most prestigious theologians in the known world, and yet she was absolutely undaunted.

On the first day of her trial, her prosecutors told her that if she made any further attempts to escape from Rouen—as she had continued to try, undeterred by her near-death experience at Beaurevoir—she would immediately be convicted of heresy. Joan rejected this statement at once, knowing that it was unlawful. She would continue to refuse to swear to tell the truth in all things, although she was forthcoming with a lot of information about the voices.

For the next several days, Joan would be questioned every day in something that resembled an interrogation more than it did a trial. Every day she would spar with the court about the oath, and every day the court would try a new angle to prove that her voices were nothing other than a hallucination, a psychological manifestation of a physiological quirk that came about as a result of her habits or health. To this day, though many experts in the medical field have studied her case, it still cannot be said where these voices came from. She was far too robust to have suffered from one of the typical diseases of the period and far too lucid to have had a recognizable mental illness.

Joan testified that the voices were still with her and that one had spoken to her on the very day of one of her sessions, telling her to "Answer boldly; God will help thee." And boldly she did answer, sometimes sassing her questioners by telling them that she had nothing to say to them or otherwise describing events or visions with a clarity and calmness that nobody could have expected. She was questioned on every aspect of her life, from the prophecies surrounding her to the visions she experienced to her campaigns and her relationships with others. Theological questions were also put to her, some of them so difficult that it was thought no peasant should be able to answer them—as many theologians could not.

One of these was "Do you know if you are in the grace of God?" In the Catholic Church, this was a trick question; to answer "yes" would be considered prideful and presumptuous, while to answer "no" would be as good as a confession to sin. Joan's answer was instantaneous and without hesitation, and it surprised the entire court. "If I am not, may God place me there; if I am, may God so keep me," she responded. Her answer left her questioners speechless.

In fact, Joan often answered with a wisdom and understanding that startled the court, and her trial became an embarrassment to the English. It could no longer be held publicly; instead, from mid-March onward, she was questioned in prison.

Now the trial began to take a turn for the worse. Although Joan did not falter, she started to realize that regardless of what she answered, she would be condemned. She started to warn the prosecutors that if they judged her poorly, God would be her protector. Delivered in her typical calm manner and with her piercing eyes, it must have been unnerving. But the judges were gaining ground, starting to find something upon which they could condemn her. They could find no evidence to charge her as a witch, but one thing was undeniable. Joan had dressed frequently as a man. In fact, standing in the court itself, she was dressed as a man as they questioned her. During that period, cross-dressing was considered a heinous crime and a sign of heresy.

As much as both Joan and the witnesses that the court questioned—among them Jean de Metz himself—argued that dressing as a man had simply been a reasonable and normal precaution, the court recognized that it had finally gotten hold of something that it could convict her for. Even though Joan protested that she was only wearing her hosen in a bid to avoid rape from her guards, the court made no attempt to defend her virginity. Instead, after weeks of trial, the court finally came to a decision. Joan was found guilty of cross-dressing. And she was sentenced to death.

Chapter 19 – The Burning of Jeanne d'Arc

"As the dog returns to his vomit," the death sentence read, "so you have returned to your errors and crimes."

Joan's calm was broken, but her conviction was not. Tears poured down her cheeks as she listened to the bishop reading her death sentence. In a moment of what she saw as weakness, she had confessed to heresy the day before, but she had quickly renounced her confession, and now it was May 30th, 1431, and she was about to be burned at the stake.

She continued to listen as the bishop read her sentence. The stake was readied, the firewood lying about its base. Eight hundred soldiers stood around her, armed to the teeth; even now, they still feared the might of Joan of Arc.

"We decree," the bishop went on, "that you are a relapsed heretic, by our present sentence which, seat in a tribunal, we utter and pronounce in this writing; we denounce you as a rotten member..."

Joan prayed quietly to herself, raising her hand to her chest to feel the tiny, hard shape of a little wooden cross that one of the English soldiers had made for her, probably from the very wood with which she was about to be burned. The shape of it reassured her a little, allowing her to stand quietly and listen to the rest of her sentence.

Then she was led to the fire. She was closely followed by Friar Martin Ladvenu, her confessor; he carried with him the crucifix from the local church, which she had begged him to bring so that she could gaze upon the face of her beloved Jesus as she burned. She wept constantly and lamented as she was bound to the stake, but she did not resist. And then, without further ado, the fire was lit beneath her. Flames licked up along the wood, roaring higher and higher, closer toward her small feet where she stood at the stake. She wore a woman's dress, but her hair was still not the usual length of the period; it tumbled, loose and dark, down her shoulders as she kept her eyes fixed resolutely on the crucifix. The flames kept rising, and as they rose, she begged Martin to lift the crucifix higher and higher. He lifted it, seeing the flames reflected in her bright blue eyes. She barely blinked, even as the smoke enveloped her.

"Jesus!" It was a scream for help or a plea for mercy—no one could say for sure, but its sheer desperation was undeniable. "Jesus!" she cried again, her tear-filled eyes still fixed on the cross. "Jesus!"

The spectators were crying; the English soldiers stood weeping as they watched Joan burn, the flames rising up to cover her body, licking at the edges of her dress, scorching up her arms and legs.

"Jesus!" Joan cried out. "Jesus!"

There was a moment of silence. Joan was hidden in the flames by now, at the very heart of the flickering blaze. Then there came one final cry. It was loud and ringing, and there was something more than fear in it. Something that could have been recognition or even joy.

"Jesus!"

And then Joan of Arc was dead.

* * * *

When the fire had died down, the English made sure to sift through the soot, looking for human ashes to prove that Joan was dead indeed, that there would be no return of France's greatest heroine. When they found her ashes, they carried them off to the River Seine, where they were tossed carelessly into the water. Floating and curling inside the waves, these little gray flakes were all that was left on earth of this bright and shining person. Her pure, high voice. Her piercing, blue eyes. Her straight posture on a horse, the ferocious determination with which she brandished her banner. It was all gone, just some gray dust now, carried off on the current of the Seine.

But Joan believed that this was not the end of the story. She believed, and she told Friar Martin, that she would be in paradise by the grace of God. She believed that she would be singing and dancing in heaven that day with the God she trusted. And after all she had suffered, after the war she didn't ask for, the treachery she had suffered, and the imprisonment that she had to endure, she still believed that the eternity she yearned for would be worth it all.

Conclusion

Statue to Joan of Arc, Paris
https://commons.wikimedia.org/wiki/File:Joan_of_Arc_Emmanuel_Fremiet.jpg

In the years following the death of Joan of Arc, Charles VII would continue to rule over France, and he grew into an able king who established one of the first standing armies in the medieval world. This move would not only sound the first death knell of the age of chivalry, which would eventually bring an end to the Dark Ages, but it also finished off his victory over England in the Hundred Years' War. Two decades after Joan died, the war would be over. France won a decisive victory, and the English were driven back to Great Britain, forced out of the borders of France for good in 1453.

Joan's name still remained on every pair of lips in the kingdom, even though her ashes had long since dissolved into the Seine. While the war was won by good military command during the later years of Charles's reign, no one could deny then—or can deny now—that the appearance of Joan of Arc brought about what could be considered a miraculous change in the war. Before she arrived at Chinon, France was undoubtedly losing the war; to the English and to Charles himself, it seemed to be only a matter of time before France would be lost. Yet France didn't lose. It won the war, and it only started winning when a strange teenage peasant girl arrived in the court of the king and convinced him that God had sent her to save his country.

Despite the fact that Joan remains one of the most well-studied figures from the Middle Ages, scientists still have not been able to pinpoint a cause for her visions. Whatever their cause, they made her one of the most legendary figures in France, a symbol of the country's national identity, and one of the first warrior women who would begin to turn the tide in a world dominated by men.

In 1452, long after her death but before the war had officially ended, Joan's mother requested a retrial. She knew full well that her daughter had died unfairly, and she couldn't bear to see Joan go down in history as a heretic. Pope Calixtus III agreed to the trial, and after three years of investigation, Joan's name was cleared in

1456. Instead, the bishop that had judged her, Pierre Cauchon, was found guilty of heresy himself for persecuting her due to his political agenda.

In the years that followed, multiple statues and other monuments were erected to Joan. Some of the places that played a key role in her life—such as her birthplace and the tower in Rouen where she was imprisoned—are still in existence and have become major tourist attractions. Statues to her stand in Paris and Orléans, among others. Multiple books and movies have been made about her, including one famous biography by Mark Twain.

Joan has also been the subject of some interesting theories, some of which celebrate her as a genius, others calling her either mad, pagan, or simply a myth. One thing that remains certain is that Joan is a mysterious figure, and many questions about her life still go unanswered by history and science. To the Christian faith, she is a symbol of what God can do through small and ordinary people.

This fact would be demonstrated a little more than a hundred years ago when Joan was officially canonized in 1909—497 years after she was born. She became known as Saint Joan, the patron saint of France. Now, a feast day has been dedicated to her, as well as a national holiday; rallying songs in the First World War mentioned her and spoke of her story, and even today, she remains a symbol of hope and inspiration.

Still, there is something a little tragic about Joan's story. In her own words, she had never asked to be a warrior maiden. All she wanted was a simple, ordinary life spinning wool in boring little Domrémy. Instead, she had to endure battles and betrayal, trials and execution, treachery and doubt. She would die a horrible, painful martyr's death at the tender age of only nineteen, condemned by the very church that she served so fervently. And yet, according to Joan, she had known what was coming. She had walked into her own death with open eyes, driven by her passionate devotion to her faith and to France.

Joan was many things: mysterious, determined, enigmatic, faithful, and undoubtedly a little bit strange. One thing, however, stands out throughout her story, running through the tapestry of her life like a golden thread. In a war that had been started by greed, when a power-hungry king decided that one kingdom was simply not enough, Joan's actions are marked by unselfishness. Over and over again, she chose a course that often resulted in pain and unhappiness for herself. If she hadn't, France might have never won the war. And history would look very, very different.

Here's another book by Captivating History that you might like

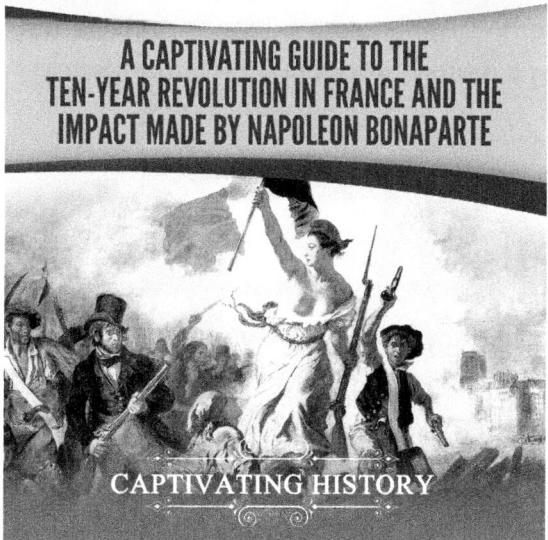

Free Bonus from Captivating History (Available for a Limited time)

Hi History Lovers!

Now you have a chance to join our exclusive history list so you can get your first history ebook for free as well as discounts and a potential to get more history books for free! Simply visit the link below to join.

Captivatinghistory.com/ebook

Also, make sure to follow us on Facebook, Twitter and Youtube by searching for Captivating History.

Sources

https://rosaliegilbert.com/births.html

https://en.wikipedia.org/wiki/Joan_of_%C3%89vreux

http://faculty.goucher.edu/eng330/ceremonies_of_homage_and_fealty.htm

http://www.bbc.co.uk/history/historic_figures/edward_iii_king.shtml

https://en.wikipedia.org/wiki/Battle_of_Sluys

https://www.realmofhistory.com/2016/05/03/10-interesting-facts-english-longbowman/

https://www.britishbattles.com/one-hundred-years-war/battle-of-sluys/

https://warfarehistorynetwork.com/daily/military-history/edward-iii-and-the-battle-of-sluys/

Illustration I: By Artistdesign - Own work, CC BY 3.0,
https://commons.wikimedia.org/w/index.php?curid=16659495

https://www.historyhit.com/facts-about-the-battle-of-crecy/

https://www.britannica.com/event/Battle-of-Crecy

https://www.britannica.com/biography/John-king-of-Bohemia

https://en.wikipedia.org/wiki/Black_Death#Death_toll

https://www.history.com/topics/middle-ages/black-death

http://www.bbc.co.uk/history/british/middle_ages/black_01.shtml

https://www.historytoday.com/ole-j-benedictow/black-death-greatest-catastrophe-ever

https://www.britishbattles.com/one-hundred-years-war/battle-of-poitiers/

http://www.newworldencyclopedia.org/entry/Battle_of_Poitiers

http://www.medievalchronicles.com/medieval-battles-wars/battle-of-poitiers/

https://erenow.com/biographies/the-black-prince/6.html

https://www.historic-uk.com/HistoryUK/HistoryofEngland/Black-Monday-1360/

https://www.history.com/this-day-in-history/hail-kills-english-troops

https://en.wikipedia.org/wiki/Bertrand_du_Guesclin

http://www.newworldencyclopedia.org/entry/Charles_V_of_France#King_of_France

https://www.britannica.com/biography/Peter-king-of-Castile-and-Leon

https://www.britannica.com/biography/Henry-II-king-of-Castile

https://en.wikipedia.org/wiki/Battle_of_N%C3%A1jera

https://en.wikipedia.org/wiki/John_Chandos#Death

https://www.britannica.com/biography/John-Chandos

https://www.revolvy.com/page/Battle-of-Auray

Illustration III: By PMRMaeyaert - Own work, CC BY-SA 4.0, https://commons.wikimedia.org/w/index.php?curid=47915747

http://www.luminarium.org/encyclopedia/hastings2pembroke.htm

http://www.luminarium.org/encyclopedia/larochelle1372.htm

http://www.englishmonarchs.co.uk/plantagenet_34.html

https://www.britannica.com/biography/John-of-Gaunt-duke-of-Lancaster

https://en.wikipedia.org/wiki/Edward_III_of_England#Late_years

http://www.newworldencyclopedia.org/entry/Charles_V_of_France#Marriage

https://www.historylearningsite.co.uk/medieval-england/peasants-revolt/

https://allthatsinteresting.com/charles-vi

http://www.newworldencyclopedia.org/entry/Charles_VI_of_France#The_King_goes_mad

Illustration IV: By John Cassell - Internet Archive, Public Domain, https://commons.wikimedia.org/w/index.php?curid=45474611

http://www.englishmonarchs.co.uk/plantagenet_9.htm

https://en.wikipedia.org/wiki/Henry_IV_of_England#Rebellions

http://www.medievalwarfare.info/#siege

https://en.wikipedia.org/wiki/Gunpowder_artillery_in_the_Middle_Ages#Advances_in_the_Late_Middle_Ages

https://www.futurelearn.com/courses/agincourt/0/steps/8857

https://blog.nationalarchives.gov.uk/blog/baptism-fire-steel-stone-henry-vs-army-siege-harfleur/

https://www.britannica.com/event/Battle-of-Agincourt

https://www.britishbattles.com/one-hundred-years-war/battle-of-agincourt/

https://en.wikipedia.org/wiki/Treaty_of_Troyes

http://www.historyofwar.org/articles/battles_bauge.html

https://www.history.com/topics/british-history/henry-v-england#section_4

Illustration V: By Unknown - Ms 6 f.243 Battle of Agincourt, 1415, English with Flemish illuminations, from the 'St. Alban's Chronicle' by Thomas Walsingham (vellum), English School, (15th century) - Lambeth Palace Library, London, UK / The Bridgeman Art Library, Public Domain, https://commons.wikimedia.org/w/index.php?curid=139585

Illustration VI: By Eugène Romain Thirion - Upload to EN.Wiki: 02:59, 19 Feb 2005 Neutrality., Public Domain, https://commons.wikimedia.org/w/index.php?curid=110523

https://en.wikipedia.org/wiki/Siege_of_Orl%C3%A9ans#Hundred_Years'_War

https://www.history.com/topics/middle-ages/saint-joan-of-arc

https://www.biography.com/people/joan-of-arc-9354756

The Hundred Years' War: A Captivating Guide to the Conflicts Between the English House of Plantagenet and the French House of Valois That Took Place During the Middle Ages, by Captivating History, 2018

https://en.wikipedia.org/wiki/Bede

https://www.jeanne-darc.info/biography/prophecies/

https://en.wikipedia.org/wiki/Hundred_Years'_War

Illustration I: By Arnaud 25 - Own work, CC BY-SA 4.0, https://commons.wikimedia.org/w/index.php?curid=53420390

https://en.wikipedia.org/wiki/Bible_translations_into_French#Chronological_list

https://www.historytoday.com/archive/joan-arc-born-domr%C3%A9my

https://sites.google.com/site/byuhistory201group6/group-project/the-lancastrian-phase

https://en.wikipedia.org/wiki/Treaty_of_Troyes

https://www.encyclopedia.com/history/modern-europe/treaties-and-alliances/treaty-troyes

http://movies2.nytimes.com/books/first/g/gordon-joan.html

https://en.wikipedia.org/wiki/Charles_VI_of_France#English_invasion_and_death

https://en.wikipedia.org/wiki/Henry_VI_of_England

https://www.jeanne-darc.info/biography/visions/

https://www.thoughtco.com/medieval-child-teens-at-work-and-play-1789126

https://en.wikipedia.org/wiki/Catherine_of_Alexandria

https://en.wikipedia.org/wiki/Margaret_the_Virgin

https://injoanofarcsfootsteps.com/articles/tag/robert-de-baudricourt/

https://en.wikipedia.org/wiki/Robert_de_Baudricourt

Illustration II: By The Life of Joan of Arc, Vol. 1 and 2, Anatole France ; http://www.gutenberg.org/etext/19488, Public Domain, https://commons.wikimedia.org/w/index.php?curid=1553037

http://www.maidofheaven.com/joanofarc_vaucouleurs.asp

https://en.wikipedia.org/wiki/Battle_of_the_Herrings

https://www.stewartsociety.org/history-of-the-stewarts.cfm?section=battles-and-historical-events&subcatid=1&histid=506

https://en.wikipedia.org/wiki/Charles_VII_of_France#King_of_Bourges

https://medium.com/interesting-histories/interesting-histories-joan-of-arc-7512922e41d0

Illustration III: By Andrew C.P. Haggard (1854-1923)modified and colorized by Rinaldum - original source: Andrew C.P. Haggard: France of Joan of Arc New York John Lane Company 1912transferred to Commons from fr:Image:Portrait jeanne d'arc.jpg, which was taken from lib.utexas.edu (original image source was here, archived version), Public Domain, https://commons.wikimedia.org/w/index.php?curid=94591

http://www.maidofheaven.com/joanofarc_quote_I_am_not_afraid.asp

https://www.jeanne-darc.info/trials-index/the-examination-at-poitiers/

http://www.indiana.edu/~dmdhist/joan.htm

http://archive.joan-of-arc.org/joanofarc_short_biography.html

Illustration IV: By Jules Eugène Lenepveu (1819 – 1898) - published on en.wiki here by User:Gdr, taken from http://194.165.231.32/hemma/mathias/jeannedarc/lenepveu2.jpg , Public Domain, https://commons.wikimedia.org/w/index.php?curid=803067

https://en.wikipedia.org/wiki/Siege_of_Orl%C3%A9ans#Assault_on_the_Tourelles_2

https://www.thoughtco.com/hundred-years-war-siege-of-orleans-2360758

http://www.joan-of-arc.org/joanofarc_life_summary_orleans2.html

https://www.history.com/topics/middle-ages/siege-of-orleans

http://www.joan-of-arc.org/joanofarc_life_summary_victoire.html

http://www.maidofheaven.com/joanofarc_patay_battle.asp

https://www.thoughtco.com/hundred-years-war-battle-of-patay-2360756

https://www.sparknotes.com/biography/joanofarc/section5/

Illustration V:
https://commons.wikimedia.org/wiki/File:Troyes_Rue_Linard_Gonthier_R01.jpg

http://joan-of-arc.org/joanofarc_life_summary_rheims.html

https://www.cs.mcgill.ca/~rwest/wikispeedia/wpcd/wp/j/Joan_of_Arc.htm

Illustration VI:
https://en.wikipedia.org/wiki/Joan_of_Arc_at_the_Coronation_of_Charles_VII

http://www.maidofheaven.com/joanofarc_reims_coronation.asp

https://en.wikipedia.org/wiki/Reims_Cathedral

http://jean-claude.colrat.pagesperso-orange.fr/2-sacre.htm

Illustration VII:

By Anonymous - This image comes from Gallica Digital Library and is available under the digital ID btv1b105380390/f144, Public Domain, https://commons.wikimedia.org/w/index.php?curid=16973390

https://www.catholic.org/saints/saint.php?saint_id=120

http://www.maidofheaven.com/joanofarc_paris.asp

https://www.sparknotes.com/biography/joanofarc/section7/

https://www.revolvy.com/page/Siege-of-Paris-%281429%29

https://www.jeanne-darc.info/battles-of-jeanne-darc/attack-on-paris-1429/

http://www.maidofheaven.com/joanofarc_jeanne_darc_autumn_1429.asp

http://www.maidofheaven.com/joanofarc_long_biography.asp

https://en.wikipedia.org/wiki/Hundred_Years%27_War,_1415%E2%80%931453#The_Anglo-Burgundian_alliance_leads_to_the_Treaty_of_Troyes

https://en.wikipedia.org/wiki/Siege_of_Saint-Pierre-le-Mo%C3%BBtier

http://www.maidofheaven.com/marktwain/joanofarc_mark_twain_personal_recollections_book2_chapter41.asp#compiegne

https://www.jeanne-darc.info/battles-of-jeanne-darc/siege-of-compiegne/

Illustration VIII: By Paul Delaroche - [1], Public Domain, https://commons.wikimedia.org/w/index.php?curid=27221

http://www.stjoan-center.com/time_line/part08.html

http://www.maidofheaven.com/joanofarc_maidoffrance_captivity.asp

https://history.howstuffworks.com/history-vs-myth/joan-of-arc-trial2.htm

https://www.jeanne-darc.info/trial-of-condemnation-index/

https://sourcebooks.fordham.edu/basis/joanofarc-trial.asp

https://en.wikipedia.org/wiki/Trial_of_Joan_of_Arc#Preliminary_inquiry

http://www.maidofheaven.com/joanofarc_feastday.asp

http://www.maidofheaven.com/joanofarc_death_sentence.asp

Printed in Great Britain
by Amazon

https://en.wikipedia.org/wiki/Joan_of_Arc

https://en.wikipedia.org/wiki/Death_by_burning#Christian_states

Illustration IX:

https://commons.wikimedia.org/wiki/File:Joan_of_Arc_Emmanuel_Fremiet.jpg